Sins *of* Neglect

Sins *of* Neglect

What It Means to Ignore Social Responsibilities

LILY ABRAHAM

One Meaning
PUBLISHING
Gilbert, Arizona

Sins of Neglect : What It Means to Ignore Social Responsibilities
Copyright © 2015 by Lily Abraham

All Rights Reserved.
No part of this publication may be reproduced, stored in a retrieval system or transmitted, in any form or by any means — electronic, mechanical, photocopying, recording or otherwise — without prior written permission from the publisher, except for the inclusion of brief quotations in a review.

For information about this title or to order other books and/or electronic media, contact the publisher:

One Meaning Publishing
PO Box 3285
Gilbert AZ 85299
www.onemeaningpublishing.com

Publisher's Cataloging-In-Publication Data
(Prepared by The Donohue Group, Inc.)

Abraham, Lily.
  Sins of neglect : what it means to ignore social responsibilities / Lily Abraham.
    pages ; cm

  ISBN: 978-0-9846824-0-9
  1. Responsibility. 2. Social ethics. 3. Conduct of life. 4. Faith. I. Title.

BJ1451 .A27 2015
170.44

Notice of Liability
This book was written to educate and inspire. Therefore, it makes no guarantees of results, expressed or implied. Neither the author nor One Meaning Publishing shall have any liability or responsibility to any person or entity with respect to any loss or damage caused, or alleged to have been caused, directly or indirectly, by the information contained in this book.

Printed in The United States of America
Cover and Interior design: 1106 Design

TABLE OF CONTENTS

1	Sins of Neglecting Yourself	1
2	Crimes of Failing to Develop Humanity	9
3	Lost Opportunities of Turning Away from Morality	21
4	Failures of Forgetting the Past	31
5	Conflicts of Rebelling Against Maturity	43
6	Dependencies of Overlooking Your Independence	55
7	Risks of Ignoring Boundaries	67
8	Mistakes of Defying Consequences	79
9	Vulnerabilities of Unconditioned Instincts	91
10	Injustices of Deserting God	103
11	Empty Promises of Avoiding Reality	117
12	Insecurities of Abandoning Your Soul	131
13	Casualties of Running from Your Battles	145
14	Insanity of Hiding the Future	161
	About the Author	177

1
SINS OF NEGLECTING YOURSELF

We hear many stories of how things hide in us. Good. Evil. Guilt. Innocence. Secrets. Needs. Wants. How do we get them to come out of hiding? How do we get to see others' true identities before they get the chance to hurt us? How do you get to see your true self before you make mistakes that hurt you?

It all depends on what you are willing to learn. What will you do with the knowledge? How will you react to what you learn about others? Are you mature and responsible enough to know people's secrets? Are you strong enough to cope with what is hiding in you?

Fears hide in all of us. We ignore them to get what we want. It is not the same as going through them. Ignoring your fears means you are acting impulsively and irresponsibly. It is acting without giving any thought to the consequences or how your actions affect others. It is how mistakes are made.

It is no secret that we all make mistakes. It is a never-ending cycle of life. We make mistakes learning what we want and do not want, what makes us angry and what makes us happy. We get hurt, and we hurt others. Mistakes are choices that affect our lives. They are choices influenced by our fears.

Ignoring your fears allows you to redefine your responsibilities in a relationship. It prevents you from learning the true meaning of social responsibility. It can teach you to neglect the shared responsibility you have for your own safety and security. Neglecting yourself in that way causes you to feel victimized and as if you have no control over it. That is why it is important for you to learn how to go through your fears and not just ignore them.

Fears play tricks on you. Fears can lie and get you to believe things that are not true. We have the responsibility of deciding if they are telling us the truth or not. Otherwise, they are like demons that torment us until the day we die.

One of the reasons we ignore our fear is because we know how relentless it can be. The problem is that when we ignore it, we learn to ignore our neglect and our sins along with it. We ignore the neglect and sins of others, too. Ignoring our fears has taught us to ignore a lot of things that happen in life that have real consequences.

Fear can scare us into doing something we know is wrong. For instance, we know it is wrong to sin, but we may not know why it is wrong. If you tell someone there are consequences for ignoring their social responsibilities, they will most likely gain an understanding of why. It forms a picture in the imagination that has real meaning for what is happening in life today.

We are taught that if you want something you need to learn how to ask for it. What happens if you experience failure or rejection? It can bring out fears we do not know how to cope with.

Fear can actually teach us how to neglect our needs and the responsibility we have for ourselves. Because fear has the power to misguide us, we have a social responsibility to gain control over ourselves and maintain it. It is a complicated and challenging process. It is where our struggles in life begin.

> Sin is something we hide in ourselves and pretend does not exist.

Going through your fears shows you what is hiding inside you and others. It reveals the sin hiding in our fears. In the past, society was taught to define sin as sloth, envy, gluttony, wrath, pride, greed, and lust. Now, in the future, we ignore sin as if it has no meaning or effect on us.

Sin is something we hide in ourselves and pretend does not exist. Ignoring it does not change what it is, the pain it causes, or where it leads to. Acting as if it does not exist causes us to lose control over ourselves when we need it most. Sin takes us down a long, torturous, complicated path that teaches us to justify hurting others, unjustly.

Sin hides in our wants and needs. It comes out of hiding when we want something. Sin causes us to rebel against society to get what we want and to ignore our social responsibility to keep others safe and secure from the damage we are capable of causing to them and their lives when we are scared.

We have incredible power and control. Because of that, we have certain social responsibilities to maintain. We need self-control before we make mistakes and then wonder what went wrong. Not many blame our problems on our failure as human beings when neglect weakens us and leads us to failure, poverty, and dysfunction.

Neglect puts us on a path toward an unknown and unexpected future. It allows sin to get control over us, and it is a fate worse than death. The power we have can turn into sin. Sloth, envy, wrath, greed, and lust are forces that can empower us to destroy lives and then neglect the consequences of it.

Neglect gives our fears an opportunity to coax us into sin and ignoring our social responsibilities. Neglect does not mean we just lie around, locked in our rooms, doing nothing. There is always activity in our lives. We still engage with others. We maintain relationships even if they are wrong for us. Our choices still affect others.

Doing whatever you want is not having control over yourself. It is a lack of control. Self-control teaches the mind and the body to work together to overcome the battles between right and wrong that we secretly fight inside of ourselves. If your neglect hurts someone, you will be held accountable by the people you hurt and society.

Our primary goal in life should be to get control over ourselves so we can get control over our lives. It is never too late to begin taking control over yourself. You are given many opportunities. It takes real courage to seize them. The challenges we encounter make it extremely difficult to do. It helps to know what is hiding inside of us to get control over it before it gets control over us.

Each of us has an individual responsibility to society that can only be realized through the control and power that we exert over ourselves and our own lives. We can change things in our lives that we have no control over by taking control over the things we can control — beginning with ourselves. Neglect hides within us: In our immaturity, in our imagination.

Our minds need to be developed. Knowledge hides inside of us, and they say that knowledge is power. If knowledge is power, what kind of knowledge? Knowledge of what? What kind of power is knowledge giving us? Is it what we need to get control over ourselves — or others?

Your life will be full of questions you need to answer. The right answers are hiding inside of you. They put you on a path toward the future. They do not magically appear. You have a responsibility to learn what they are, and it takes time and effort. They hide behind all your fears, and confronting them is the only way to get to the answers you need.

Knowledge is a power we can fail to use correctly. It can bring emotions out of hiding that we have never experienced before and have no control over. Learning provides us with knowledge that teaches us how to get control over ourselves. Knowledge feeds into our imaginations. It changes what happens inside of us — in our minds, in our imaginations, and in our bodies.

Fears provide us with knowledge. For that reason, fears need to be included in the thought process. It is how we learn about the many things we do not know about ourselves and others. The truth is hiding in our fears. Ignoring our fears prevents us from learning the secrets hiding in all of us.

Experiences and relationships show us who we are and give us the opportunity to learn about ourselves and our fears. We have a responsibility to learn so we can avoid making mistakes. They cause varying degrees of damage to our identity and our lives. The damage is repaired with the clarity that comes from learning about our fears, and using that learning to avoid making the same mistakes in the future.

Unfortunately, clarity is difficult to acquire when we lose sight of ourselves and our own actions. There are many unknowns that cause us to lose our way in life. Finding our way back becomes a painful journey — it can take us deeper into denial about who we are.

We gain knowledge about ourselves in many ways, especially through our memories, after we have made a mistake. When we do something wrong, our memories do not let us forget it. They can be painful. Fortunately, we can find our fears hiding in them. Tapping into that knowledge allows us to reach our full potential.

Being good is not like being innocent. We are not good until proven evil. We have to prove ourselves to society. There is more evil hiding inside of us than good. And it has made itself invisible. We have to prove that we have control over ourselves and that we are not going to lose it when we do not get our way.

Having control means preventing yourself from making the same mistakes that are caused by fear over and over again.

Having control prevents your choices from leading to the same disastrous results over and over again. Having control means showing compassion and understanding when others make choices that impact your life.

Learning self-control means learning about ourselves so we have the power to succeed. Learning is a strength or power that defines our character. Neglect gives sin power and an opportunity to inspire and motivate us to do the wrong thing. Learning gives us the power to resist sin and neglect and seize the opportunity to do the right thing.

Because we are human and do not always know what the right thing to do is, God devised a plan to guide us past all of our sins and the mistakes they cause. Neglect interferes with our control, and the secrets hiding inside of us cause dysfunction. Social responsibilities create a path that teaches us right from wrong so that does not happen. All we have to do is learn.

2

CRIMES OF FAILING TO DEVELOP HUMANITY

Our future begins with seeing something we want and taking the first step toward getting it. That step tells others what our intentions are, and relationships begin to form. That one step alters our lives in ways we can never imagine.

Our actions take us on a journey to a destination. We do not always see where we are going. Yet, we always manage to end up somewhere. Our journey begins with the knowledge that is in our head. All minds receive thoughts and inspiration. It is the most private and secluded place on Earth. It is where neglect begins without anyone being aware of its existence.

It is our own neglect that gets us into trouble. Attraction is a powerful force that can cause us to forget about everything and everyone. It can control our behavior and dominate our imagination. It causes us to neglect our responsibilities.

Neglect is the evil — not attraction. Because neglect gives attraction such a bad name, there is much debate over right and wrong. With a clear understanding of neglect, we can see that some rights and wrongs are not debatable. They are what they are, and we have no control over it.

Our choices lead us to people we can trust and people we cannot trust. There is a right way and a wrong way to ask for what we want. There is right way and a wrong way to react if we do not get it. It all depends on whether people can be trusted or not. Our reactions reveal our success in developing humanity or our failure to develop it.

Right and wrong exist to create and maintain order. We all have needs, and it is our responsibility to satisfy them according to what is right and wrong. Right and wrong were defined centuries ago. It is a reality we cannot avoid. Redefining it causes conflict and disrupts the order established by society to provide for our collective needs.

We have a need and a responsibility to prevent conflict from ever becoming a reality. We have a responsibility to keep our battles over right and wrong confined within us, in the privacy of our own minds. That is difficult to do without humanity.

Being human means that everything we do is inspired by thoughts that secretly flow through our minds. It is easy to ignore right and wrong when we want something. It is easy to ignore the conflict it causes. It is easy to keep that neglect a secret inside of us. As humans, we have a responsibility to become conscious of it.

It is no secret that disagreements over right and wrong cause conflict with others. What is a secret, hiding inside of us, is how we react to conflict. How do you react to people you disagree with? Do you see your fear of them? Or do you see your judgment of them? The fear is hiding in your judgments.

Ignoring that fear can prevent you from developing humanity. Fear influences our beliefs in right and wrong. People will use their beliefs in right and wrong to deny us what we want and to get what they want. It does not mean they are evil, or doing something wrong. Our judgments of them tell us when we lack understanding of who they are and why they do what they do. Without that understanding, conflict erupts.

Conflict is inhumane. It is unexpected, and it goes against our nature. Yet, people continuously disagree, loudly and publicly — sometimes to shame people they believe have wronged them. It is something we have no control over, and because of that, conflict causes anxiety and paranoia. It instills uncontrollable fear in us. It prevents us from knowing what to do, and it delays choices we need to make.

Conflict is time consuming and emotionally exhausting. Not everyone does the right thing, and they tend to keep it a secret when they do the wrong thing. Some do the wrong thing so often that they develop a visible habit of neglecting their needs and responsibilities. At that point, it is no longer a secret, and it becomes your neglect that puts you at risk if you choose to ignore it. People who neglect themselves will neglect you, also.

When we ignore right and wrong, we ignore our needs and responsibilities. It allows us to put sole responsibility for our safety and security on others and society. Doing the wrong thing causes us to neglect the needs of others and our responsibility for their safety and security. We fail to develop trust in our relationships, and it causes us to lose control over ourselves and treat others inhumanely.

Trying to trust someone who is neglectful leads to disrespect, and there are consequences for that. Disrespect prevents you from developing humanity. You develop humanity by doing the right thing and through the trust that follows. That means if you want to develop your humanity, you need to place trust in people who can be trusted — people who are worthy and deserving of your trust.

Trust is a reward for developing humanity. Trusting people is a choice you need to make of your own free will, rather than out of habit. It is not an easy choice to make. If you are wrong, it will be painful. You will suffer as a consequence. Doing it of your own free will allows you to think before wrongly trusting others, blindly and faithfully. As humans, we need to take responsibility for our own safety.

Failing to develop humanity alters our understanding of right and wrong. It leads to conflict and distrust. We see the conflict before we see the distrust. Distrust is an evil that hides in us. The things we want prevent us from seeing what distrust does to us, and it can lead to inhumanity that is extremely difficult to get control over.

Humanity is something that hides within us and prevents us from fighting with others. It is not as simple as being kind, caring, and compassionate. It is hard to be kind, caring, and compassionate when you do not trust someone or are angry with them. Anger dehumanizes and demonizes you, causing everything you do to be misunderstood.

Holding on to your humanity can be a struggle. The meaning of it has evolved as a result of all the injustice running rampant around the world. Because of all the wrongs in life, our need for humanity has never been greater. Anger divides us, and we have no control over that. Ignoring it will not teach us how to make things right.

When we want something we can try to hide our anger and pretend it does not exist. That kind of neglect robs us of opportunities to develop humanity. We all have guilt, and we all keep it a secret while we learn how to move past it. Our actions lead to success or failure. We do things wrong before we do them right. We make mistakes.

It would be difficult to find anyone who has not been victimized by someone's mistake. When we get angry we have a responsibility to be understanding of the choices that are made by others. It teaches us civility.

> Humanity is a social responsibility that separates us from animals.

Evolution is demanding we find the humanity within us and learn to act better than animals that kill each other just to stay alive. While there is much debate over where humans came from, there is evidence that suggests we came from animals. You can see it in our behavior.

However, regardless of our beliefs, reality is giving us overwhelming evidence and proof that we are humans. Even if we did begin as animals, it does not justify our acting like one. Without humanity, we allow our animal instincts to surface and take control over us.

Animal instincts are inherent in us, and neglecting that fact has consequences. When we act like animals, we are treated like animals. Wild animals do not survive among society. They are either killed or captured and kept in a cage. It is not a future we envision for ourselves. Something we want leads us there.

Animals fight for dominance and control to survive. Failing to develop humanity causes us to do the same. As humans, we have the responsibility to learn how to rationalize our anger so we develop our ability to communicate with words and actions that express respect, not the anger we are feeling. Social responsibilities are a form of communication that expresses our will to survive, respectfully.

Humanity is a form of communication. We communicate it through respect. Our ability to communicate with each other through our learning and responsibilities separates us from animals. It conveys our intentions and allows others to see the good hiding inside of us. We have a responsibility to allow others to feel safe around us.

We do not trust animals until after we have disciplined them. We train animals to have respect for us. We have a responsibility to show each other the same respect we demand from animals. As humans, we need discipline before we can be trusted.

Learning respect is a discipline that develops our humanity and trains our minds and instincts to respond to it. It disciplines the mind and body to work together. It provides us with the ability to learn a skill that provides us with the means to acquire food and shelter for ourselves and avoid conflict.

Humanity is a social responsibility that separates us from animals. We have the capacity to gain an understanding of civility through our beliefs in right and wrong. Our minds have the ability to discriminate between choices that lead to success or failure, with only the hope of a reward.

Learning humanity is how we learn what we know and do not know about trust, respect, and civility. Learning from it conditions our instincts and turns us into rational humans. Rationalizations are a human trait and provide us with knowledge to gain an understanding of life that goes beyond just acting for a reward that may or may not be waiting for us.

We all need food, shelter, and discipline. Laws, rules, and boundaries exist to give us guidance so we do not neglect our needs and responsibilities. Failing to develop our humanity can teach us to turn to a life of crime just to get what we want in life.

Neglect causes us to cross the boundaries of humanity to get what we need to survive. Being human does not give us the right to lie, cheat, and steal from others. Being human means we have the responsibility to learn self-discipline. Being human means we have a brain that can learn. Being human means we have the ability and, therefore, the responsibility to learn how to take responsibility for ourselves.

Being human means we have responsibilities we cannot ignore. As adults, we need to compete to stay alive. We have the responsibility to give something in exchange for it. Responsibilities are a medium of exchange. Promises are a medium of exchange. Exchange is another word for responsibility.

We make promises in exchange for responsibilities so that we can survive. We have a responsibility to live up to the promises we make to others in exchange for our survival. It is the humane and civil thing to do.

Civility and respect are part of our humanity. They are necessary for our survival. Without it, we will kill those who get in the way of what we want, and, eventually, all of society will perish. Humanity is essential to our evolution.

No one can force us to evolve, and no one can prevent us from devolving, either. We can devolve right under the nose of society and hold it responsible for neglecting us. The lack of humanity will justify punishing society when we feel wronged because of it.

Because of neglect, we recognize guilt in others before we see it in ourselves. It requires respect and civility to gain an understanding of it. We need humanity to prevent ourselves from lashing out at the pain our own sins and neglect cause. Humanity is holding ourselves responsible for being wronged, not society.

Beliefs in right and wrong teach us to foresee the rewards and punishments associated with our actions. Right and wrong lead us in two entirely different directions with very different opportunities. Right attracts people and opportunities we can trust. Wrong attracts people and opportunities we cannot trust.

Our humanity inspires others to willingly give us what we want, without having to demand it or issue threats. Doing the right thing builds trust in relationships. Doing the wrong thing breaks it down.

Neglect teaches us to communicate through fear and various forms of aggression that can scare people. Your fears can cause you to act aggressively to get what you want. Fear can be used to exert influence over others. It is not a means of asking for what you want. It is a means of overpowering people who have what you want and demanding it or taking it from those who may be unwilling to give it to you.

Neglect is an invisible force that can take control over you and your life. You need discipline to prevent that from happening. When neglect takes over your life, all you can think about is what you want and learning how to get it. You obsess and lose control. It causes you to act inhumanely around others and in society.

Our humanity is developed by gaining an understanding of what it means to be human. We have a responsibility to earn what we need for our survival. Nothing given to us is free. Sometimes, all others ask for in return is respect. Those who give to us worked hard for what they have, and they choose to share it with others. They have earned respect.

Disrespect puts us on the path to inhumanity. Disrespect allows us to believe it is wrong to force discipline on someone, or to force them to take on responsibilities in exchange for their survival. Disrespect allows us to believe it is wrong to expect someone to do something that does not feel right or natural to them. Disrespect creates an intense desire and willingness to be neglectful, and allows us to believe it is a right that society has a responsibility to respect.

Neglect can feel natural. It can feel like a freedom we are entitled to. It is a freedom we begin exercising with the things we want. It is a freedom that causes us to ignore our need for humanity. We are not born with humanity. It is a learned behavior that guides us through life and keeps people safe and secure.

Conflict can cause you to feel deep down in your soul that you are doing the right thing when, in reality, it is wrong. If your actions lead to you losing control and becoming a threat to your or society's safety, security, or freedom, it is wrong. It takes humanity to see that neglect is a threat to all of that. Aside from all the pain it causes, neglect deprives you of what you need to survive, prosper, and be happy.

Responsibility and neglect are mortal enemies that need to fight it out inside of us. Neglect is a constant threat to our ability to take responsibility for ourselves. We are all capable of learning skills to survive. We are all capable of developing our minds and taking control over ourselves. Choosing responsibility over neglect is how we learn humanity and what it truly means to be human. It is not easy, but it is possible.

People who fail to develop humanity do the wrong thing or, worse, commit crimes of their own free will. They believe the right thing to do is to just let everyone do whatever they want to do, without consequences. Criminals believe they should be able to do whatever they need to do for their survival, without consequences. Failing to develop humanity causes us to feel wronged by consequences.

Feeling wronged can cause you to destroy someone and their life and lead you to believe it is the perfectly right thing to do. Murderers feel their actions are justified. Killing can feel natural to some people. All of this begins with a disagreement over right and wrong. Does the lack of humanity make it right?

3

LOST OPPORTUNITIES OF TURNING AWAY FROM MORALITY

If your future depended on your ability to be moral, would you have what it takes to survive? Or would evolution bury you alive? People who do not learn how to confront their fears get left behind. Morality hides in our fears. It is difficult to do the right thing when you are being pressured to do the wrong thing and too scared to do the right thing.

Immorality can cause you to feel dead inside later in life. It is a slow death caused by disappointment gradually eating away at your happiness. You can feel as if you and your life are buried alive beneath all your shattered hopes and dreams. Our lives today were inspired by the morality that existed in the past, not our hopes and dreams. They can shatter and destroy us in the process.

Your actions tell others what your priorities are. Doing the wrong things tells them that living is not one of them. We need to learn how to survive before we can live. We learn by doing the right thing. Life is full of possibilities and opportunities when learning is a priority.

Doing the wrong thing once is all it takes for it to influence the path of your future. All habits begin by doing something once, even bad habits. If your behavior is rewarded, you will continue to do it, repeatedly. You will have hopes and dreams of receiving the same rewards over and over again.

Doing the wrong thing does not mean you are immoral, but it can put you on the path toward it. Morality does not come naturally to anyone. It just comes easier for some. It is a learned behavior, just as humanity is.

Morality is easy to neglect because it is often misunderstood. It is misinterpreted as a form of self-deprivation. It causes us to fear that we will not get what we want in life. That fear can be the first of many that misleads us.

Many see morality as a religious thing when it is actually a relationship thing. Because religion teaches it, we believe we have a choice in whether we learn it or not. While many believe that religion is a choice we can ignore, morality is a choice we need to make of our own free will.

Morality is not learned by all of us. However, it is taught by all of us. We may not even realize we are teaching it. Whenever we feel wronged, we expect others to learn how to do the right thing of their own free will.

Turning away from morality causes our relationships to be built on distrust. That distrust leads to sin. Not being able to trust someone leads to pain and anger. Immorality is letting sloth, envy, gluttony, wrath, pride, greed, and lust get control over you. It has a bad habit of destroying people and their opportunities in life.

Morality is a social responsibility that teaches us how to govern our own behavior. It is not self-deprivation. It is self-discipline. We know what is going on inside of us, and we have a responsibility to take control over it.

Morality is making responsibility a priority over everything. Morality is about taking control over yourself to prevent anyone or anything from getting control over you. Learning morality is taking responsibility for becoming a productive and functional member of society.

The path to failure begins with us neglecting to learn who we are and what we are capable of. Morality prevents the things you want from distracting you while you learn. It teaches you *how* to manage your responsibilities without depriving yourself of what you want. With morality, you learn to conquer your fears by providing for the needs that are triggering them.

Our thoughts and emotions guide us toward the choices we need to make. We cannot rely on attraction alone to guide us. The activity in our minds provides us with the information we need to make informed decisions. The decisions we make are life altering. Lives have been known to fall apart because of wrong choices.

Attraction can cause that to happen. The things we want can cause us to make bad choices. It is something that makes us human. Attraction exists without any effort on our part to control it. It is important that we take control over it and let it guide us without distracting us from our responsibilities in life. We have goals to pursue, and attraction can interfere with our pursuit of accomplishment.

Right and wrong has evolved into a system of rewards and punishments. Its original meaning is to give us clarity on the paths to success and failure. Our responsibilities require more of our attention and focus with every passing year. Rewards and punishments teach us how to get control over ourselves as we travel the path toward prosperity.

We need prosperity to live and not just merely survive. That requires us to have others' trust and respect. Morality is learning to be worthy of it. People need to know you can be trusted with responsibilities. Privileges are the reward for being trustworthy. Responsibilities create a path to those privileges. If you want the privileges that come with morality, focus on the responsibilities leading up to it.

Morality has evolved into a social norm that is expected of us. There are many things society considers normal. An education is one of them. Learning makes you normal. It is more than a path to a graduation with a high school diploma. It comes to your defense and defeats the fears you have for your survival.

Our survival is dependent on our ability to earn an income and maintain that ability throughout our lifetime. An education gives us personal and individualized guidance. When you apply yourself to every subject you are taught, you learn your strengths and weaknesses. Others will push and pull you toward what they want. Knowing your strengths and weaknesses will tell you what you need, and you can push or pull yourself in the direction you need to go.

Our primary responsibility as children is to get an education. It is when society begins putting trust in us. It teaches us how to use our mind and focus our imagination on doing the right thing. It is a big responsibility for a five-year-old, but that is when neglect begins. Responsibility needs to begin when we are children to prevent neglect from influencing our beliefs as adults. If kids are focusing on colors, letters, and numbers, they are less likely to get distracted later in life.

We need to learn how to get control over our minds from an early age. It gets more difficult and complicated to do as we age and mature. At some point, it can become impossible to do. Neglect begins in childhood. It forms habits that lead to immorality later in our lives.

Learning teaches us habits that lead to maturity and independence. Habits form early in our lives. They are controlled by our opinions and judgments, which inspire our imagination from a very early age. They affect our beliefs in right and wrong. It is never too early to begin forming good habits. The older we get, the harder it gets to break them.

"Morality" is a word that defines a behavior and an attitude. It is a habit that forms inside of us, based on the belief in doing the right thing for the right reasons. Morality teaches us to be honest with ourselves and others. It teaches us how to take control over ourselves, not others. That is difficult to do if you do not know how to discriminate between right and wrong. Sometimes we need to go back to the beliefs we were taught as a child to learn the difference.

We learn to talk at a very early age. Talking is easy. Learning to communicate is challenging. Communication is another social norm. Have you ever thought about what would happen, or not happen, without it? It is responsible for everything that happens. It is responsible for everything we hope to gain from our efforts. We would have nothing without it.

Communicating effectively to avoid misunderstandings is difficult and complicated. An education develops and strengthens our ability to communicate. Morality affects the way we communicate our needs and wants to others. It teaches us to communicate clearly to avoid unforeseen complications later in our lives.

Words alone do not show others what you are capable of doing, or what you will do in the future. Learning communicates that. It validates your words and builds trust. An education reveals the options and opportunities you will have in the future. Learning morality is a step toward that. Turning away from morality leads to lost opportunities.

> **Doing the right thing prepares you for success and prosperity.**

We can pretend to get an education. We can go to school every day and pretend to listen to what teachers are teaching. We can get failing grades and blame it on the teachers or on the materials they use. We can blame it on the school's budgets or financial resources. Rarely do we blame it on ourselves and our lack of focus and attention — the very definition of neglect.

Pretending to do the right thing is immoral and the wrong thing to do. Doing the right thing prepares you for success and prosperity. Doing the wrong thing prepares you for a life of failure and poverty, with no opportunities to change it.

Doing the wrong thing causes you to fear things you should not fear and to not fear the things you should fear. It causes you to fear and distrust morality. Many people do the wrong thing because they fear that doing the right thing will deprive them of what they want.

Our survival begins with *wanting* to survive. Morality does not take that away from us. Learning how to survive needs to be a priority. We need to learn how to survive before we can survive. There are things we need to do before we get what we want.

Turning away from morality teaches us how to escape the responsibilities and opportunities that morality prepares us for. Choosing to learn morality of our own free will teaches us how to take responsibility for our own safety and security so we can protect our freedom as human beings.

Morality prepares you for opportunities and relationships in your life. Doing the right thing rewards people. Doing the wrong thing punishes them. Immorality teaches people to distrust you, and it puts your safety and security at risk as a consequence.

We can neglect our own safety and security by regarding our happiness as a priority. An education does not need to be fun.

It needs to be effective. Our needs and responsibilities can rob us of free will and prevent us from doing what we want to do. Sometimes we need to do things we do not want to do. We can deprive ourselves of something we need to be happy because we are too focused and busy chasing after something we *think* will make us happy.

Morality gives our needs an opportunity to surface so we can focus our attention on them. Neglecting our needs weakens us and breaks down our will, causing us to struggle throughout our lifetime. Morality teaches us to see the attractions we feel as an incentive to keep us strong and give us something to work toward.

Immorality teaches us how to use attraction to mask the pain of neglect. The things we want can hide the pain that neglect causes. Doing the wrong thing can be rewarding, but the rewards are a distraction that cause us to turn away from morality and the opportunities it attracts.

Turning away from morality means turning toward something else. The lack of a high school education means finding another way to survive that is not socially acceptable. It allows attraction to lead you away from the responsibilities you have. It gives the things you want control over you and leads to immorality and sin.

Sloth, envy, gluttony, wrath, pride, greed, and lust are known as the Seven Deadly Sins for a reason. They are forces that can prevent you from doing what you need to do to survive. They can prevent you from keeping your promises and living up to your intentions. They can cause you to fail to live up to society's expectations.

Sin is a manifestation of fears and needs that get ignored. While it is part of being human, we have a responsibility to prevent it from getting control over us. Sin interferes with our ability to remain functional and productive. The forces that drive us to immorality are real and extremely powerful. They are difficult to resist. If it was easy, religion would not have any reason to forewarn us about them.

4

FAILURES OF FORGETTING THE PAST

The past shows us the role that humanity and morality play in our lives. Evolution has clearly shown us the future they create. Society was taught a very long time ago that immorality forces us to keep secrets that cause us to self-destruct. Forgetting that will cause us to fail in getting control over ourselves and our lives.

Immorality is not a simple belief in doing the wrong thing. It begins as a belief that you can communicate your needs through the things you want without having to learn morality. It allows you to ignore your fears and act impulsively to get what you want from others. Your fears make it difficult to foresee your needs being different than what you want.

Chasing after what you want actually causes you to neglect your needs when you fail to get what you want. When you do not get what you want, you do not get what you need. It allows your desires to get control over you and prevents you from learning what you need to know about yourself and others before acting. Ignoring your needs leads you down the path of neglect to failure.

The paths to success and failure were defined in the past. Since they are relevant to our survival, they are taught to us. Forgetting what was taught about failure in the past will lead you directly to it.

Failures matter. Not getting what we want is failure. If we do not prevent ourselves from making the same mistakes over and over again, we will never get what we want or what we need for the future. Everyone has a past. We will not have a future if we forget the lessons learned in it.

Success and failure have a voice in our lives that speaks for us. They communicate with others. They tell them how we spent our time and what we have put our mind and efforts into. They show them what we did right and what we did wrong in the past.

Many believe the past is a place to hide our mistakes. It is a common burial ground for guilt. The problem is that you cannot bury the past and forget it when it is very much alive in your memories. The past is full of choices you made, right and wrong. You had your reasons for making them. There are things you wanted to happen and things you wanted to prevent from happening. There were things you knew and things you did not know — until now.

The past is just as much a part of our lives as the future is. Our pasts are unique. That means no two are the same. Because of that, no two futures are the same. Our pasts are a valuable resource for learning who we are and what we need to survive. It provides us with all the knowledge and power we need to get control over ourselves for the future.

We all have different fears, different needs, different weaknesses, and different strengths. We all have different lessons to learn that are specific to our goals in life. All of it affects our judgment of right and wrong. What is right for one person can be wrong for another. Your past can give you insight into what is right and wrong for you — and nobody else.

Your failures hide in your past. Our failures like to hide, and we want to forget them. They are secrets we try to safely bury in our memories.

We tend to remember being victimized more than we remember our failures. Many of us feel we have been victimized at one time or another by someone. Being victimized is a consequence of failure from past choices. We tend to place blame solely on the people we believe wronged us. It is a habit that allows us to neglect our own actions, and it is a habit that is hard to break.

Misplacing blame is the reason we make the same mistakes repeatedly or habitually. Habits are behaviors we repeat without giving any thought to them or to where they lead. We just assume we are not doing anything wrong, and it can start fights.

Habits lead to conflict before they lead to success or failure. Habits can be traced back to the things we want. Sorting through past conflicts can help us learn the role our habits played in our failures.

The past can show us the things we need to stop wanting and stop acting on. The past shows us who we rewarded — and why — to get what we wanted. We learn whether they were deserving of it. If they wronged you, it was wrong to reward them. That is a mistake that needs to be corrected. It is something you have control over and can stop doing.

Forgetting the past will lead to failure, repeatedly and habitually. Remembering it and learning from it provides you with knowledge that can change your future. It teaches you what you have control over and what you do not have control over. Learning the difference will give you control over your life and lead you to a life that is right for you.

The past holds many secrets. The future happens naturally, as a result of choices you made in the past. It is a time of immaturity and impulsiveness. You can see what you wanted and what you got as a result of choices you made and people you trusted. It shows you where you neglected your needs and responsibilities to give you an understanding of why you did what you did and the influence others may have had over you.

The past gives you insights into what you need to survive. It is a time of learning humanity and morality. It is a time when learning to take responsibility for your safety and security is a priority over learning how to get what you want. Impulsiveness puts you at risk in relationships.

We learn from our past through memories. Your reactions to people and experiences hide in your memories. Your past is full of pertinent information that is valuable to you and the life you want to build. It is not a garbage can for everything bad that happened to you, or because of you. Mistakes live on in our minds long after we think we have moved past them. We cannot hide our past from anyone — not even ourselves.

Everything we do leaves a trail. It allows us to find our way back to where it all started. Reflecting on the past shows you where you lacked control over choices you made and outcomes you share responsibility for. The futures we foresee are not guaranteed. A lot happens between now and then that you have no control over.

The past can reveal the fears you ignored to get what you want. It is the time to develop a habit of listening to what your fears are saying to you. It develops your human instincts and prepares you for all the unknown and unexpected events in your future. It teaches you how to get control by relying on human instincts that are developed through fear and foresight.

We need control over ourselves to achieve success. We are always thinking ahead. Our past is filled with hopes and plans for the future. Imagining our future influences the choices we make. Foreseeing the wrong future leads to mistakes that cannot be undone, damage that cannot be repaired, and failures that will never be forgotten.

We rely on foresight for every choice we make. It is limited by what we are willing to learn. Life is full of unknowns that only our fears can make us aware of. We learn things that scare us. That fear is an opportunity to expand our intelligence and sharpen the instincts that lead us to the future. Intelligence affects every aspect of our lives. It controls every human function.

We put hope in our imagination that allows us to be optimistic about the future. We see fear as negativity that attempts to sabotage all of it. All those fears we ignore as negativity are warnings. They are truths that provide insight into others' imaginations. It shows us what others want and need and when it may be different than what we want.

We misinterpret insight as fear and pretend it is not relevant to our choices when, in reality, it has the power to decide our future. Ignoring others' needs puts your future at risk. You have no control over others, or what they need and want. A relationship holds you responsible for satisfying them.

Your fears are designed to prevent you from acting impulsively, to give you an opportunity to gain insight into your own needs, and to prepare for the responsibilities that follow. They give you time to foresee all the possible outcomes of choices you make and those that others make. They give you the opportunity to get to know others who may have more control over the future than you do.

Our futures can shatter years before we get to them. Hard work and persistence is not going to hold our future together if we do the wrong thing in the past. As we learn about ourselves, we become more aware of our differences with others. It can lead to conflict putting us in a position of vulnerability.

The past shows you your strengths and weaknesses. Your weaknesses bring out fears of rejection and failure. People will judge you every day of your life. Judgments are not the evil that destroys our lives. Ignoring them is.

Fears of rejection and failure can cloud your judgments and bring out a desire for acceptance. It can interfere with your attempts to develop the necessary skills you need to survive. Your strengths hide inside of you. Getting an education with the intent to earn an income allows you to focus on your strengths and protect yourself from those who will judge you based on your weaknesses. Getting an education for any other reason negatively influences society's judgment of you and alters your future.

An education is about receiving validation, not acceptance. It is a time to learn if you are learning what you think you are learning and what you need to learn. It is a time to correct your mistakes if you are wrong. Success is built on that validation.

> **Failure sends us back to where we started — alone and lost.**

Society puts us on the path toward success and prosperity. Choices you made in the past reveal your aspirations and motivations. Accomplishments show your ability to learn and take control over yourself. In the future, you will be judged on your ability to handle responsibilities.

Your past communicates what you have learned and accomplished. The past is for learning who you are through your strengths and weaknesses. A desire for acceptance can lead to a history of failure. It can distract you from learning how to succeed and prosper.

Desires are a force we cannot repress. Learning to manage them and maintain control over ourselves is a vital step toward our survival. Acceptance is not just something we want. It is something we need, in the future. That is why there is a socially acceptable path toward it.

Chasing after it will cause you to fear for your safety and security in the future. Your safety and security is a privilege that comes with responsibilities. Your future is dependent on others' judgments of you, and yours of them. You cannot ignore them and hope for the best. Their judgments can cause the worst to happen and lead to your failure.

Your survival depends on your ability to keep the promises you make. Taking control over yourself is never the wrong thing to do. Being human means we will make mistakes. The things we do not want to happen are more likely to happen than the things we want to happen. Being human does not excuse us from the damage it causes or the consequences that follow. The future will hold us responsible for the pain and damage that neglect causes.

It is your responsibility to prevent your neglect from following you into the future. Failure sends us back to where we started — alone and lost. Neglect is not something you can hide in the past, or ever forget. It haunts you till you overcome it.

Filling your past with accomplishments supports the choices you made. You may never get to where you want to go, but you will end up somewhere. Accomplishments will give you something to show for your time and efforts. They ensure that your past will not be a complete waste of time and not worth remembering.

Learning morality means it will take longer to get where you want to go. But, in the meantime, you learn to trust and be trusted. If you have time to do something wrong, you have time to do it right. Making mistakes means spending time correcting them in addition to learning morality and how to do things right.

Forgetting what you learned in your past will lead to failure in your life and in your relationships. We cannot make mistakes and then ignore them as if they never happened. We cannot keep going as if we were making the right choices. Mistakes change things.

Our fears of rejection and failure are strongest when we are immature and impulsive. Our reactions to our fears can dictate our future. Accomplishments give you the power to conquer them.

Morality allows attraction to work for you, not against you. Attraction is pulling something toward you. Why waste time and effort chasing after something that you can pull toward you? Delaying satisfaction of the things you want teaches you how to attract them to you. You do not need to chase after acceptance. Focusing your attention on an education prepares you for opportunities you are drawn to. Success attracts people who will accept you in the future.

Plan your past. Foresee the future you want, learn what you need to do to get there, and do it with morality. Planning your past and filling it with accomplishments means having a past you will never want to forget. It will lead to a future you know and are prepared for. You will not feel alone and lost in the future if you learn to communicate your needs through past successes.

5

CONFLICTS OF REBELLING AGAINST MATURITY

"Grow up." It is a common expression used to resolve conflict. What does it really mean? What are we doing that compels someone to say that? Why is it so difficult to resolve conflict maturely? Why is our first instinct to rebel and maintain our "immaturity"?

Conflict means that someone is right and someone is wrong, in the mind of the accuser. Who is wrong? The person who is immature — or the one who is impatient with someone's immaturity? Is placing blame the mature and responsible thing to do? Do we have a social responsibility to punish people who are wrong?

There is a more effective and efficient way to resolve conflict than by growing up. Maturity takes time, and most people do not want to wait that long to resolve their differences. We have become a society that wants satisfaction, immediately.

Placing blame does not solve a problem. It identifies a problem and raises questions on how to resolve it. Life is full of questions that only maturity can answer. Getting there is not easy or simple. One question can lead to many different answers with varied outcomes. Getting to maturity requires answers that lead to many more options and choices. We get to where we want to go one right choice at a time.

Choices were made in the past, and they were not always the right ones. They have forever impacted our lives, and the effects will outlive all of us. The path to maturity has changed because of wrong choices made by our ancestors. Evolution is exposing all of the lies, deceits, betrayals, and sins of the past. Neglect is no longer a secret we can keep buried. It is very much alive inside of us and altering our beliefs in right and wrong.

People with maturity know what immaturity looks and feels like. They have been through it to get where they are. Maturity is a path we all travel. It reveals the differences between us and others. One of those differences is authority.

Authority is a major cause of conflict and rebellion and even more conflict. Authority is knowing the differences between right and wrong with certainty. Differences are not problems that can be resolved. They cause problems that need to be resolved. Knowing what you want gives you certainty in your own life, not the authority to tell others what is right for them.

We know what we want, and we believe we have the authority to go after it. When people get in our way, deprive us of what we want, or do the wrong thing, it creates adversity. Authority is a power that makes people angry. Adversity is not an evil. The impulse to punish someone for it is an evil.

Adversity teaches us to enforce rules and boundaries that can seem unfair or harsh. It does not mean we have to agree with it, but we do have a social responsibility to respect it. Disrespect is a form of rebellion. Our first instinct can be to punish people we disagree with to teach them respect. That urge hides our need to learn respect from them.

People with authority can see the immaturity in others through the negative emotions it stirs up in them. Inhumanity and immorality hide in immaturity. It causes fear and anger in others that will cause them to use their judgments to deprive you of what you want from them. It teaches you maturity.

Maturity is not always learned from authority. Immaturity can teach us to rebel against learning it and make it easy for us to refuse to conform to social norms. It is difficult to sustain relationships when we do not get control over the beliefs and emotions that trigger rebellion.

Emotions can control our reactions. Immaturity is acting on an emotion that is going to pass. Reactions should be based on logic and intelligence, just as our actions should be. Emotions can cause us to see punishments as a way to put an end to someone's behavior. It will hurt them. But what will it do to you and your future?

Rebellion means doing the wrong thing. It is an impulsive behavior controlled by the fear that maturity will somehow change your identity. Immaturity prevents you from seeing that rebellion alters the way people see you. It has an adverse effect on your identity and prevents others from getting to know who you truly are. Rebellion leads you away from what you want and prevents you from learning skills to cope with the changes maturity does make in our lives.

Instead of spending time and effort in fighting against maturity, that time could be better spent forcing yourself to do the socially responsible thing. Maturity is a social responsibility. Adversity forces us to make choices we do not want to make. It forces us to do things we do not want to do. It also alerts us to changes we need to make in our lives so we can stay on our intended path toward the future we want.

Respect is the solution for the problem of adversity. Respect gives us the opportunity to get control over ourselves and prepare for choices adversity forces us to make. Respect is not the surrender it appears to be. It is a form of self-control that buys you time to open your mind to understanding the differences between right and wrong when emotions are strongest.

We need more than courage to confront the fears that have surfaced because of all the pain caused by our struggles to deal with adversity. We need forgiveness. It is another form of self-control that prevents us from avenging ourselves. We do not acquire humanity and morality because others treat us with it. It is the result of choices we make based on our ability and maturity to forgive.

You cannot have maturity without learning humanity and morality. They are needed in times of adversity. Resolving conflict requires sacrifices that can bring out all kinds of fears and negative emotions. Humanity and morality teach you how to grow up and deal with it.

Adversity causes fears. Do not dismiss your fears by throwing them to the back of your mind and forgetting them. Throwing negative emotions to the back of your mind and holding the positive emotions in the forefront is immaturity. Instead, raise your awareness of others' needs. It is the mature thing to do in a relationship.

Dividing your emotions into positives and negatives means you are conflicted over what the right thing to do is. Conflict can gradually change your feelings toward someone. During that time, your actions say things you do not want them to say, and your words lose meaning.

Positive and negative emotions need time to fight it out inside of you. Positive emotions will tell you what you want. Negative emotions will tell you when you are not getting it. Being deprived causes conflict inside of you and in your relationships. You have a responsibility to learn maturity and prevent that conflict from escalating.

Doing the right thing is often done under protest. Immaturity has a way of making the things we need to do challenging. We cannot rely on positive emotions to guide us to where we want to go, and rely on negative emotions to tell us what to avoid. Regardless of how well we think we know ourselves, emotions can be deceiving and misleading — even positive ones.

Emotions go through a maturation process. Negative emotions reveal true feelings you are neglecting. They allow you to get what you need from others through dishonesty that later leads to disrespect. They prevent you from being honest with yourself about what you want and what you need.

Life has rules. Following them expresses maturity. Right and wrong is about honesty and dishonesty. It is about responsibility and neglect. Acting with dishonesty is immoral. It is wrong to ignore negative emotions just because they cause us to fear we will not get what we want.

Immaturity is a time of uncertainty. Maturity is about making choices that are right for you. It brings out fears and insecurities. If you rebel against maturity, those fears stay hidden inside of you. It causes them to strengthen in intensity and, eventually, destroy you, your relationships, and your future. Hidden fears make life a living nightmare.

Immaturity is a painful time in our lives. Immaturity is an evil we all battle inside of us. It is a powerful force that can get control over us in ways we cannot imagine. It causes us to make mistakes and to rebel against rules and responsibilities. It causes confusion over right and wrong. It causes us to struggle when learning to discriminate between our wants and needs.

The past is your path to your maturity. Your struggles should lead to accomplishments. Rebellion leads to struggles that lead to nowhere. We think it leads to change, but it is only leading to conflict. It tells us that there is a lot about life that we do not understand. There are secrets and mysteries we cannot even begin to comprehend until we learn to understand what is going on right inside of our own minds and bodies.

Growing up is painful. Our pain is healed through our forgiveness of those who teach us how to grow up through adversity.

We have a social responsibility to fight against immaturity and all the pain it causes. Maturity reduces our risks of being victimized. Finding acceptance with our true feelings is difficult when it is not how we want to feel. But, there are times when it is how we need to feel to keep ourselves safe.

Confronting our emotions gives us the maturity to deal with life. It gives us clarity on how to interact with society. Life is full of opportunities and possibilities. That means we can walk away from a relationship and what we want and still survive. It takes maturity to prevent conflict and maintain peace.

It is more effective and efficient to walk away from conflict than it is to wait for someone to grow up. Conflict teaches them maturity, and there are no guarantees they will learn it. Not everyone can make the sacrifices they need to make to hold a relationship together.

Maturity does not always resolve conflict. As we age, our emotions get stronger. Anger becomes a bigger part of our lives. We need control over ourselves regardless of the emotions we are experiencing at any given time. Emotions come and go. They change minute by minute. We cannot trust them to hang around indefinitely.

Maturity is measured by your judgments. Your judgments are influenced by your successes and failures, which are influenced by choices others make. Adversity can be to blame for your failures. As unfair as it may seem, you are still responsible for maintaining control over yourself and resolving the problems it creates in your life.

It is easier to blame others for all of our problems than it is to blame our own immaturity. Immaturity is an evil that affects the way we deal with adversity and authority. The temptation to rebel against others as punishment can become too strong to resist, causing self-control to become an extremely difficult choice to make.

Every choice you make has an effect on your life and on your identity, beginning with your choice to show others respect. Understanding teaches you how to manage your emotions. Fear and anger are a natural response to the things we do not understand. Understanding makes our choices easier.

> Immaturity is a rebellion against your own survival.

You can believe that one act of rebellion will not make a difference, but you can be wrong about that. One act of rebellion is one step in the wrong direction. People have been known to get lost on that path and never find their way back. They just keep going and going until they are gone.

Immaturity is a rebellion against your own survival. Every act of rebellion diminishes your chances of becoming a functional and productive member of society. Disrespect is an evil that gets inside of you and is extremely difficult to eradicate. It digs deep into your soul and grows roots. It causes damage that is difficult to repair. It has negative effects on your identity, character, and humanity.

Respect is not about earning merit badges or brownie points. It is about earning an income for your survival. Maturity is something that is taught to all of us through adversity, whether we like it or not. If we learn it willingly, we can control our actions and reactions. We can get control over the changes that happen naturally in our life as a result of choices we make.

We have a responsibility to live up to our full potential as human beings. We have a responsibility to set goals and work through the challenges that come with them. It gives us clarity on our future. Goals give you guidance to a future specifically designed to satisfy your needs and wants.

Your needs and wants will change with maturity. Maturity changes everything that needs to change in you and in your life. Those changes give you more clarity on your future and how to maintain peace in your relationships. What made you happy in the past may fail to make you happy in the future. Pursuing your goals teaches you who you are and what you need to be happy in the future.

CONFLICTS OF REBELLING AGAINST MATURITY

It is wrong to rebel against our maturity just because it makes changes in our lives. It is wrong to simply go through life doing only what we want to do. Getting what we want involves sacrifices and patience.

Maturity is something that hides inside all of us. It is just waiting to come out. It hides behind rebellion and anger over adversity. We do not always get time to think before acting. Self-control prevents us from acting on impulses and emotions that impact our entire future. Immaturity makes it difficult to comprehend the full meaning of neglect and the failure it leads to.

The responsibility to do the right thing follows you throughout your entire lifetime. Maturity is a process. It happens in stages to give you time to learn respect and adapt to all the changes your responsibilities force you to make in your life. When the process is complete, maturity allows you to maintain your true identity.

Maturity gives you independence. Respect is not easy or simple to learn. It is one of many lessons we need to learn on the path to maturity. No one ever said that growing up was easy or fun. It is a path paved with anger and disappointments. Disrespect is impulsive and caused by undeveloped instincts. Respect sharpens and matures your human instincts so they alert you to choices that threaten your identity and independence.

6
DEPENDENCIES OF OVERLOOKING YOUR INDEPENDENCE

When you think of freedom, do you think of happiness? It is easier to chase after happiness than it is to attract it. Waiting for it is confusing and frustrating. What do you do in the meantime?

It is difficult to live your life without happiness. The impulse to chase after everything we see and think will make us happy gets stronger when we are unhappy. In the meantime, do not let unhappiness prevent you from taking responsibility for your safety and security. Do not let it justify impulsive behavior. In the meantime, learn to get control over yourself.

Not getting what we want makes it even more difficult to maintain control over ourselves. At some point in our lives, we become aware of the unfairness and injustice in life. You will witness others' success in getting what they want while you continue to struggle through life. It is times like that when we lose control, and envy takes over. Everything that follows afterwards can become a blur.

Chasing after what we want causes us to lose sight of the future our choices are creating. Boundaries and responsibilities become blurred. Things we do not want to do may be the things we need to do. Getting what we want is not always the path to happiness. Ending our struggles is. We cannot do that by neglecting our responsibilities.

Doing what we need to do will make us happier in the future than doing what we want to do now. It requires us to exert control over ourselves. Being independent means doing what we need to do on our own, without someone forcing or coercing us to do it against our will. Independence is knowing what the right thing to do is on our own, and doing it of our own free will.

The path to independence can be deceiving. It is not as easy or as simple as it appears. It is complicated, and it began many, many, many years ago.

Things happened in the past that we do not understand. Therefore, our ancestors were not able to pass down that understanding to us. We have a responsibility to learn on our own. Evolution is just now getting around to teaching us what we need to know for the future and our independence.

DEPENDENCIES OF OVERLOOKING YOUR INDEPENDENCE

Acquiring independence causes us to struggle in ways we cannot foresee. Our choices do not always lead us to where we expect them to. Our future will be out of our control if we do the wrong thing, knowingly or unknowingly. The things we need to learn for control come from our struggles to be independent.

Anyone can get what they want. But how many want it after they get it? Many times, it is not what we expected and it fails to make us happy. Then there are the times when it is what we expected, and we fail to hold on to it after we get it.

Independence is not given to us. It is learned through choices we make. Dependencies give us the freedom to ignore our needs and responsibilities while we chase after what we want to be happy. Overlooking your independence causes you to form dependencies on others for what you need to survive. That means you will not be able to survive without them.

We are born with needs, not the ability to take responsibility for them. As humans, we do not spend a lot of time focusing on our needs. When we need something, it seems to be there for us without us having to ask for it. We do not spend time learning how it got there or why it is there.

What if, sometime in the future, you need something that is not there for you? What if you cannot accomplish your goals or survive without it? How will you react? With humanity or without humanity? It is not easy to prevent our emotions from influencing our choices.

We are constantly making choices that require maturity and morality. We get torn between what we want to do and what we need to do. Persistence in getting what you want does not always pay off. In the meantime, you can die trying to survive.

Our needs and responsibilities grow, multiply, evolve, and mature. They are a constant in our life that we can depend on to teach us the right thing to do. Taking responsibility for ourselves can become burdensome and leave us feeling drained and exhausted. That is when perseverance pays off.

We cannot have independence without success. And success means taking responsibility for ourselves. And that means learning to take responsibility for the needs we are born with. Success frees us from our parents. But, before we can be truly free of our parents, we need to end our dependencies on them, before we carry them into other relationships.

Parents have hopes and dreams for their kids. Because of that, in addition to providing for their needs, they shape and mold their social identities by trying to contain their immaturity. As a result, it is natural for immaturity to hide inside of us and express itself through our independence. It can cause damage

DEPENDENCIES OF OVERLOOKING YOUR INDEPENDENCE

we do not know how to cope with and changes we do not know how to adapt to.

Leaving our parents forces us to depend on society for what we need to survive. Taking our dependencies with us out into society can sabotage our lives and our relationships. Because we are not taught to see them, we unconsciously ignore their existence and hide them in the back of our minds. Dependencies hide in us until relationships become threatened, or end.

We develop hopes and dreams of our own that can conflict with what others want or expect of us. When people expect you to be someone you are not, it can pressure you to make choices out of fear of being rejected. It is then that your dependencies start peeking out of the shadows of your mind.

Conflict causes us to fear that a relationship will end and that we will lose everything. That fear prevents us from learning who we are and what we are capable of doing on our own. It can lead to dependencies that cause us to doubt our identities and what we have to gain in life. They get stronger the longer we neglect our need for independence.

Conflict is an opportunity for us to be honest with ourselves. Relationships make our choices more confusing and complicated, not easier. Confronting your fear of being alone can guide you to making choices that are right for you. Independence gives you control over choices you need to make.

Dependencies teach you to ignore your needs and put others' needs ahead of your own. They give others control over you and create feelings of oppression. As wrong as oppression may be, attaching a label to it will not change your responsibilities in it.

Oppression is not the evil it appears to be. Dependencies are the evil we need to be on the lookout for. Dependencies hide behind feelings of oppression. Dependencies are a threat to your independence, and oppression is the punishment for it. The only person you should be dependent on is *you*. People die, and relationships end. What will that do to you? Can your future survive without them?

Independence has evolved into a social responsibility. It gives us the ability to survive outside any and all relationships. Dependencies are a form of laziness or neglect that cause us to become not just a burden but a threat to others and society. Forming dependencies on others robs them of their independence, and they will hurt you just to break free of you.

It is no secret that people make us happy. The problem is that they can also make us unhappy. Fearing for your safety and security is a sign of dependency. Negative emotions tell us when we are neglecting our own needs.

DEPENDENCIES OF OVERLOOKING YOUR INDEPENDENCE

Fear does not allow us to discriminate against who we form dependencies on. We can form dependencies on people who lack humanity, morality, and maturity. Those are things we cannot force anyone to learn. Rewards do not give it to others, and punishments do not teach it to them.

People who lack humanity, morality, and maturity do not take responsibility for their own safety and security. They cannot be trusted to take responsibility for yours. Dependencies allow you to trust the wrong people just to keep relationships together. There is nothing to prevent anyone from becoming a threat to your safety and security, except you.

Dependencies cause you to overlook your independence as a way to escape all of your unhappiness. Independence is like a superpower that frees us of sin and all the pain and punishments of bad choices made in the past. Independence and happiness are a moral and karmic justice that comes from making choices that free us of our dependencies.

Independence comes with responsibilities you need to prepare yourself for. It is about getting control over yourself so you do not develop a need to rely on others for guidance in your life. Independence affects your social well-being in ways that are difficult to foresee. Your ability to act responsibly, of your own will, influences society's judgments of you.

Independence is about developing the ability to take responsibility for yourself mentally, physically, emotionally, psychologically, and financially. Freedom does not give you the right to neglect all of that. Neglect causes you to struggle in unforeseeable ways. You have sole responsibility for preventing yourself from doing the wrong thing or anything that deprives you of your freedom.

Our minds have the freedom to travel and explore all the possibilities that life has to offer. We have the freedom to create a future with our choices and our own free will. Options force us to make choices that bring out the biggest fears hiding in us. Having to make choices others disagree with can be overwhelming and cause those fears to strengthen our dependencies on them. Disappointing others can scare us more than taking risks with our independence.

> Independence can be a scary thing.

Maturity and independence do not mean we will choose correctly or wisely. There is always the possibility we will make a mistake that will haunt us for a lifetime. Independence can be a scary thing. It is where fear tests our beliefs. Independence leads to struggles before it leads to happiness.

DEPENDENCIES OF OVERLOOKING YOUR INDEPENDENCE

Independence is often confused with freedom. Independence is learned. Freedom is earned. It is also a right you are entitled to, but so is everyone else. We can misinterpret and misunderstand our rights before gaining the maturity to grasp their true meaning. The conflict that immaturity causes, in the meantime, puts us at risk.

Our risks in life can be minimized by learning social responsibilities. Focusing on our rights can distract us from it. Dependencies can teach us how to get control over others instead of ourselves. Independence requires you to set boundaries for yourself to prevent that from happening.

There are many things that can interfere with our plans and alter our futures. Freedom does not give us the right to control everything and everyone in our path. Independence is taking a shared responsibility for your own safety and security, and allowing others the freedom to do the same.

Everything that happens in your life begins with you and the choices you make. You cannot depend on others to make choices that are right for you. They will do what is right for themselves.

If you want to be successful, learn to respect people who have already achieved success and independence. If you express an ability to learn, people will trust you to think for yourself. As adults, we are responsible for the choices we make.

Whether we realize it or not, by the time we become adults, we have spent our whole life learning what we want and do not want, like and do not like, and what we believe and do not believe. Adulthood is where we learn what our future will be, based on everything we learned about ourselves in the past.

The things we need to do are harder than the things we want to do. The things that are easy to do, do not always lead to what we expect. They can lead to an unknown future. Our needs have an unexpected way of leading to experiences that teach us to "grow up." Over time, responsibilities will give you what you need and attract the happiness that you believe can come only from getting what you want.

Dependencies can cause pain that prevents us from foreseeing the future correctly. Even though it may appear as if getting what you want is the only way to end the pain, independence is the solution. The comfort you foresee can be deceiving. Getting what you want can actually strengthen your dependencies and intensify your feelings of oppression.

Feeling oppressed means you lack the maturity and foresight to do what is right for you. Independence is the ability to think and act for yourself. Attracting the happiness you want is easier when you can accurately foresee the future you are creating. Prevent the pursuit of happiness from interfering with that vision. Let your priorities and responsibilities guide you. Our responsibilities can attract happiness. Our responsibilities can guide us toward a future that is right for us. The future is not as unpredictable as we think it is. We have the ability and the freedom to learn how to foresee it. It is a freedom that comes from learning independence.

7

RISKS OF IGNORING BOUNDARIES

It is obvious we are not the first people to walk this Earth. Boundaries were set centuries ago by our ancestors. What is not so obvious is that we cannot change them now simply because we are being deprived of what we want. We have what we need to ensure our survival. Ignoring boundaries can take all of that away from us.

The dictionary can define the word "boundaries," but that does not mean it has any meaning for us. It does not define all the various types and functions of boundaries out there in life and in our relationships. We need to learn what causes them to exist and the effect they have on us if we want to achieve success and prosperity.

Boundaries have a different meaning in our imaginations than they do in the dictionary. In our minds, boundaries are invisible lines that stand in the way of what we want. Becoming conscious of them raises our awareness of ourselves and the needs of society. It is wrong to focus solely on what we want and ignore what others want. Society has needs that boundaries protect. Crossing them causes pain and suffering.

When people think of boundaries, they think about staying within them, or crossing them. Not many think about learning from them as a way to get what they want from others. Part of keeping yourself safe is by expanding your boundaries through goals you set for yourself and cooperation with people who know more about what they need than you do.

Getting what you want from someone requires trust. Others need to trust you before they will establish a relationship with you. You need to prove you will not cross boundaries that threaten their safety and security and put them at risk of losing control over themselves and their lives. It requires self-control.

Humanity, morality, maturity, and independence create social boundaries. We cross or ignore those boundaries to get what we want, quickly. Ignoring them will not redefine right and wrong. It will not shorten the path to success and prosperity. Nor will it eliminate the responsibilities we have for ourselves. Ignoring them puts you at risk of losing control over yourself.

Ignoring boundaries puts our humanity, morality, maturity, and independence at risk. We need to take the time to learn them. They are resources every human needs to succeed and prosper. Dependencies place boundaries on us that we need to expand. Failing to do that leaves us powerless to set boundaries with ourselves and the people who hurt us.

Immaturity and dependencies are character flaws that do not simply pass with time and age. They are the result of habits instilled in us at birth. Over time, with neglect, they become bad habits that are rewarded every time we get what we want. It is a threat to our relationships and puts our futures at risk.

As we age, inhumanity, immorality, immaturity, and dependencies evolve into challenges we have a responsibility to overcome with hard work. They threaten our ability to get control over ourselves. It is difficult to restrain yourself and end bad behavior when it is rewarded, even if you do know it will put your social identity at risk. Boundaries were established to keep us safe from ourselves.

Ignoring boundaries causes damage that is difficult to see at the time. Hindsight gives us clarity — after the damage is done. Past neglect has forever changed our path to the future. Independence holds us responsible for setting boundaries for ourselves to overcome our challenges. It clarifies right and wrong for us.

When we envision our future, we do not see boundaries that hide in our imaginations. Those boundaries are real and hide in our relationships. It takes time to become conscious of them. Boundaries that reveal our limitations hide in our fears. Ignoring them puts us at risk of becoming a threat to others' safety and security. Boundaries put restrictions on our freedom so we do not violate others' rights.

Boundaries are established naturally by our likes and dislikes, wants and needs, what provides us with safety and security and what does not. There are rules for getting what we want and need. They vary depending on what you want, need, and who you ask.

Rules are not always spoken or taught. Some are learned through our experiences and relationships. Some are learned through respect, self-control, and social responsibilities. Some are learned through honesty and integrity. The older we get, the more rules we are expected to know and obey. It is the path to gaining trust from others and expanding our boundaries in society.

The choices we make create a path toward the things we want. It is easy to respect the boundaries that allow us to get what we want from others. It is difficult to respect boundaries that allow others to deprive us of it. It is difficult to respect others and their choices when we fear for our safety and security. Disrespect causes boundaries to become blurred when we want something. It causes power struggles that lead to conflict.

We are able to justify everything we do. Our understanding of freedom can make boundaries seem obsolete. Justifications cause us to believe everything we do is right. However, the problem with believing that we are right is that it can prevent us from getting what we need. Our needs can hide in the things we do not want, and we may need the cooperation of people we disagree with to get it.

We need boundaries to function and define our role in society. We get an understanding of our needs through boundaries. They teach us to provide for needs that surface through goals we set for ourselves.

Goals cause us to encounter boundaries set by others. People with morality and maturity have set different boundaries for themselves than those who lack these qualities. People with intelligence and prosperity have set different boundaries for others than people without them.

Every time we ignore our fears to get what we want, we are ignoring boundaries set by others. Fears define those boundaries for us. Our choices lead to events and people in our lives that we have no control over. When we ignore the boundaries defined by fear, we blindly cross them without knowing what to expect.

Confronting our fears gives us insight into what exists outside our boundaries. We can clearly see the many things that happen when we cross boundaries. People get angry. Conflict erupts. Relationships end. People refuse to give us what we want and need from them. But what about the things we cannot see? Things can spiral out of control and take us down with them.

Everything that is happening now gives us foresight into how others will react to choices we make. There are risks with ignoring boundaries. The threats to our safety and security are real. They lie outside the boundaries of humanity, morality, maturity, and independence. Acting outside those boundaries makes us a threat to others and their lives.

When people get hurt or angry, their pain knows no bounds. Crossing boundaries causes others to lose control and become unpredictable. It can trigger the worst possible outcome.

Wanting something does not give you control over others. It gives them control over you. Wanting something provides us with the perfect opportunity to get control over ourselves. Resisting the urge to act impulsively teaches self-control. Ignoring social boundaries leads to punishments — not rewards — that put you at risk in relationships.

Others' reactions teach us to set boundaries for ourselves. We choose to learn either cooperation or rebellion. They are habits we form inside of us that become visible as we mature. Choosing to ignore boundaries through rebellion puts us at risk of not getting what we need to survive.

We can become immune to the teachings of society when they interfere with what we hope to gain. Bad things happen when we fail to set boundaries for ourselves. The pain and suffering that follow mean we lack clarity on what we truly want from others and what they are willing to give.

Growing up, our relationships are personal. As adults, they are professional. We are expected to behave maturely, responsibly, and intelligently. People with maturity form professional relationships with people who live up to their expectations.

We have more freedom in our personal relationships than we do in our professional ones. People with authority are consumed by their responsibilities. Time places boundaries and constraints on us. There is only so much we can do in an hour, in a day, in a lifetime. People need to trust that you will not rebel against them and disrupt their lives. Depriving them of what they need crosses boundaries.

Promises hide in every choice you make. You are not just making choices for yourself. You are also making promises to others. They expect your honesty and integrity. People expect you to know what you say you know. They expect you to do what you say you can do. They expect you to be honest about what you do not know and cannot do.

Keeping the promises you make contributes to your success and independence. It is difficult to do when you are scared or when your choices do not lead to the happiness you were expecting. Breaking your promises is seen by others as a loss of control over yourself and a breach of trust.

There is power and knowledge hiding in our fears that can prevent us from crossing boundaries. We can learn how to expand them to protect our relationships and ensure the safety and security of others. Fears expose your mind's limitations. They reveal things you do not know, things you refuse to learn, and things you do not have the maturity to understand. Fears mean that the knowledge you have stored away in your mind puts you and others at risk.

Expanding boundaries means attracting people and opportunities that you are prepared for. Knowledge is intelligence that expands the mind's boundaries. Intelligence expands our abilities and what we are capable of doing. It leads to trust, and trust expands our boundaries in relationships.

Instead of seeing boundaries as a hindrance or an obstacle, learn to see them as options or opportunities. Doing the wrong thing creates the risk of them being closed off to you. Doing the right thing opens up your imagination to possibilities that are only limited by your limitations.

Rules tell us what we need to learn. Boundaries protect the opportunities and resources we need for our survival. Learning social responsibilities shows that we have respect for society and the opportunities and resources it provides for us. The mature thing to do is learn what those boundaries are.

When we ignore boundaries, we run the risk of being deprived of what we need to survive. Boundaries establish order and maintain peace. If we want to survive, we need to stay within boundaries that do not violate the rights and freedoms of society. Boundaries teach us what to expect from choices we make and to trust our intelligence over our emotions.

> Our wants and needs define our personal boundaries.

The more intelligence you acquire, the more fears you conquer, the more boundaries you expand. Boundaries are the result of fears society encountered in the past. Promises get broken and trust gets betrayed in relationships. We can allow our fears to scare away people and opportunities. Or, we can allow boundaries to educate us and prepare us for our responsibilities in life.

Boundaries divide society and create competition. Staying within boundaries established by society teaches us how to maintain our innocence and remain competitive. Society has defined boundaries that guide us through our fears and give us the freedom and knowledge we need to achieve individual success and prosperity.

We can survive and prosper breaking the rules and ignoring boundaries, but what kind of future does it lead to? Nothing in life is guaranteed, including success and prosperity, but learning boundaries gives us our best possible chances of attaining trust and respect. Evolution is showing us how respect affects our chances in life.

We spend so much of our life learning one thing or another. It seems to never end. The mind has limits to what it can learn and absorb, and respecting boundaries gives us time to learn what our limitations are.

Our wants and needs define our personal boundaries. Learning what we want and need simplifies our lives and makes our choices easier. Life is easier when we learn to respect social boundaries and prevent ourselves from crossing them to get what we want.

Independence gives you the ability to set boundaries for yourself and others. Learning from existing boundaries in life teaches you how to establish order and maintain peace in your life. Boundaries that exist today show you what you need to protect, and why. They defend our rights to our safety and security.

Judgments of right and wrong create boundaries that place limitations on us. Our understanding of right and wrong expands as we mature. It teaches us to be more forgiving of others. Just because someone hurts us, it does not mean they have done something wrong. It means a mistake was made in the past that only foresight of the future could have prevented.

Mistakes get made when we cannot see past today or tomorrow. People who hurt you are putting their needs before yours because it is the right thing to do. You need to learn to do the same. Our needs extend out till the day we die. It is difficult to see when that day is and everything that will happen before then.

Boundaries create comfort zones. Stepping outside our comfort zones is not always rewarding. Boundaries give us a place to return to after failure and rejection wound us. Returning to boundaries established by society comforts us when we need to get control over ourselves. Feeling deprived and neglected can cause us to lose motivation for doing the right thing when we are angry or hurting.

The whole point of setting goals is to arrive at some desired destination. The whole point of boundaries is to give us guidance toward the achievement of those goals. Goals expand our intelligence by giving us clarity on our needs and responsibilities. They define boundaries for us and reveal our limitations in society.

Goals allow us to see a beginning and an ending in our imaginations. We foresee the future we want, and goals provide the means to take us there. What happens in between depends on the choices we make in the meantime and the choices others make.

Goals are about fitting in somewhere. They show us where we belong. Accomplishments teach us how to depend on people for our safety and security without forming dependencies on them. Fears of rejection and failure will surface and test our character. Respecting boundaries influences society's judgments of us and the choices they make regarding our future.

Social boundaries create a path that provides employment and other resources society needs for its survival. Ignoring those boundaries causes us to trespass on others' rights and freedoms. It puts our future at risk by putting us on an unknown path with boundaries that lead to unexpected consequences we cannot escape.

8

MISTAKES OF DEFYING CONSEQUENCES

Boundaries exist because of human actions that threaten society's safety and security. We have learned how to communicate through our actions and through boundaries. Do you know what your actions are saying? Boundaries teach us to communicate through consequences so that we can learn. Ignoring boundaries says you do not need their protection from consequences.

Consequences are often unexpected and seen as the bad things that happen to bad people following bad choices. Rather than seeing bad choices as an evil, consequences are seen as an evil we need to eliminate. We cannot control everything that happens. So why should we be punished for it?

Bad things can follow good choices, too. The reality that bad things happen to good people disproves the theory that bad things happen only to bad people. It proves there must be other causes for consequences and all the bad things that happen besides our character and personality.

Consequences are easily misunderstood and misinterpreted. According to *The American Heritage Dictionary*, the word "consequent" is derived from a Latin word meaning *follow closely*. Consequences are the events that follow our choices and actions. Something happens, and something follows. Everything that happens is caused by something that happened before it.

What happens before a mistake is made? We can see the bad things that follow after them. But before a mistake is made, choices are made. We foresee consequences and make mistakes by defying them. We see something we want, ignore the consequences, and choose to go after it. It is not until much later that we can learn it was a mistake.

In reality, we clearly see what follows closely behind choices we make. In our imaginations, we see what happens before we make choices. We put thought into the actions that get us what we want. We avoid putting thought into the consequences or the bad things that follow. If we look closely inside our minds, and are honest with ourselves, we can see that there are a whole lot of things going on inside of our minds that we ignore before mistakes are made.

Consequences are clearly visible in our imaginations through foresight. They can take years to become visible in reality. The past taught our ancestors lessons that they failed to learn. If they had learned them, we would not be experiencing the consequences of their mistakes now. Ignoring our fears and defying the consequences causes us to make mistakes, and the conflict is still rippling through time.

Our ancestors taught us to ignore our fears a long time ago. They believed fear was an evil that prevented them from achieving their goals. They are not alive to see the consequences. It was a mistake that has divided society in many ways. As a result, we see consequences as fear and ignore them. That is how we defy consequences and mistakenly choose actions that cause our worst fears to become a reality.

Consequences are the result of choices. They cause us to act and react. Something always follows. Something always happens before them. We cannot go back in time and undo any of it. All we can do is adapt to the unforeseen and unexpected consequences of choices made in the past. Going forward, we can choose to foresee the consequences of our choices and take action based on what we foresee happening, rather than on what we *want* to happen.

We all have the ability to think for ourselves. We all have the ability to do what is right for ourselves and others. It does not mean we all have the ability to discriminate between what is right and wrong for ourselves or for others. When we do the wrong thing, we do not always know or believe it is wrong. It is why we make the same mistakes over and over again.

We know we make a mistake repeatedly because we get the same bad outcomes over and over again. If your life is not going as you planned, you would be wise to accept the guilt and not place blame on others, expecting them to correct it. The past is showing us that placing blame on others does not resolve the problem. It is our way of ignoring it.

Defying consequences does not give us control over people or events in our life. It does not give us control over the influence others' choices have over outcomes, now or in the future. Defiance has the power to influence our choices. It does not mean they are right. History can show us that defiance causes us to be wrong again and again. It has the power to create a never-ending pattern of mistakes and outcomes that become predictable.

When it comes to consequences, we need to learn to expect the unexpected. Consequences, like fears, are a resource that we can use to guide us to success and prosperity. They provide us with knowledge of how to prevent bad things from happening that are under our control. There are unforeseen consequences to all the bad things that happen. The problems they cause will not resolve themselves by our ignoring them.

Life follows a plan. Yours should, too. The life you want should follow closely behind as a result of your choices. If it doesn't, you have made a mistake. Consequences remind you of what you hoped to gain, and what you had to lose. They remind you of what you want and need.

If you did not get what you wanted, fighting over it will not change what happened in the past. It will change what happens next. Conflict becomes a predictable outcome in our relationships that consumes our minds and distracts us from getting what we want and need. Avoiding conflict leads us to tough questions about other choices we could have made.

Consequences bring up questions you did not have the answers to in the past. What are your fears telling you to learn? What can you learn from your actions? What are consequences telling you to avoid doing? Those answers should be a part of your plan.

You have a responsibility to know what outcome your actions are attracting. What will your choices attract? Not everyone respects boundaries. People and events we attract into our lives can interfere with the achievement of our goals. They can distract us from success and prosperity. The mistakes and failures it leads to are consequences of choices we make and others make. The bad things that happen tell us when we need to set boundaries in our lives and in our relationships.

There is knowledge and power hiding in boundaries. Boundaries allow us to foresee the consequences of our choices before we make them. Knowledge of consequences gives us real power over choices that affect our entire lives.

Our choices attract people, experiences, opportunities, events, and resources. They lead to more options and possibilities we may not be able to foresee. We need to learn to foresee all possible outcomes of every choice we make. One choice can be the cause of many things that follow, good and bad.

Success does not follow all goals. It does not just happen regardless of how much time and effort we invest in them. We have consequences to remind us that failure is always an option. It is difficult to recognize. It hides in the consequences that we see as fear and ignore. We defy the consequences and ignore failure by believing nothing bad will happen.

Unexpected consequences usually appear in some form of failure and rejection. They are unexpected because we ignore them when we foresee them in our imaginations. It is difficult and painful to imagine them becoming a reality.

Bad things happen when you have enemies. Bad things happen when someone sabotages your plans or goals. Bad things happen when people do not agree with you. Bad things happen because of society. Bad things happen because of others. Bad things happen because of you. Bad things happen because we do not stop them before they happen.

Bad things happen because of neglect and defiance. Bad things follow sin. We cause bad things to happen because we do not get what we want. The reasons bad things happen are endless. At this point in time, they do not matter as much as our reactions to them.

Actions can scream neglect, and we still ignore them. It is wrong to blame others when we have a responsibility for the choices we make. Guilt is not as obvious as it appears to be. We are capable of hurting ourselves and others and denying it. We have the ability to cause consequences in ways we cannot even begin to imagine — all because we have learned how to close our minds to our own failures and neglect.

We hide our failures by redefining our mistakes as opportunities to learn and try again. We can redefine our wrongs as rights. We can blame others for bad outcomes and take credit for the good ones. Having a habit of defying consequences leads to the mistake of denying responsibility for our failures and the consequences that follow.

We can do a lot of things in our minds that no one can see us doing. It is wrong to just ignore consequences and hope for the best. Failure is an ending to a choice made in the past. Mistakes will not lead to the future we are expecting.

The future is an outcome or a consequence. It follows choices we make. Consequences that happen between now and then tell us it is a mistake to allow defiance to influence choices we make regarding the future. They can reveal the neglect inside of us that is causing us to ignore others' needs and the pain it causes.

You may be able to justify your choices, but that does not make them right. Consequences are capable of causing varying degrees of discomfort. Not getting what we want brings out the inhumanity, immorality, and immaturity hiding inside all of us that can actually lead to dependencies as a consequence for making mistakes. It does not belong in relationships. Defying consequences will not make it all go away.

> Ignoring the truth has consequences.

Mistakes wreak havoc with our self-esteem. They cause pain that alters our understanding of people, relationships, and experiences. Ignoring consequences allows opportunities to appear more rewarding than they are. It puts us at risk of failure and rejection.

Everything that happens has a cause and an effect. Our choices cause something to happen, and it has an effect on us. When fear and defiance influence the choices we make, our mistakes get bigger over time and the discomfort intensifies.

Confronting our fears is a process, a period of transition. Fear confuses us. Knowing what to do takes time. Hiding our fears in the back of our minds teaches us to control the events in our lives so we can create desired outcomes. After we get what we want, all the fears and insecurities we are hiding in the back of our minds escape and move to the forefront, ready for battle and to defy all the odds against us.

Changes need to happen within us before outcomes will change. Foreseeing all the options and all the outcomes, good and bad, gives us an opportunity to think and reflect on the past and the future we are creating. It allows our needs to come to the forefront of our minds. Real change comes from becoming conscious of them and the consequences that our fears prevent us from seeing and putting thought into.

Our needs should always be in the forefront of our minds. Fears of rejection and failure cause us to ignore them and lead to our failure to take responsibility for satisfying them. There are real consequences for that.

Fear and insecurities warn us when we are not prepared for what follows next. Mistakes are the result of things we did in the past without foreseeing the correct outcome of our choices before we acted on them. Fear can warn us when we are ignoring something we need to be aware of. Focusing on our needs can change an outcome.

Mistakes bring out all the fears and insecurities hiding inside of us, and it causes conflict in our relationships. That conflict is the consequence of past mistakes that did not get resolved to our ancestors' satisfaction. We have been forced to live with our ancestors' past mistakes and all the fears and insecurities they caused. We are still fighting the same predictable battles, and the discomforts of their past failures still haunt us through our fears.

We can see the pain and suffering they endured. It does not have to be that way for us. There are many rewards in relationships, but there are also many risks hiding in them. Consequences give us insight into the risks that are inherent in every relationship. Truth hides in those insights. Ignoring the truth has consequences.

We live in a society where failure is not tolerated. When you go out into the world, you are dealing with people who do not care if you live or die. They are not related to you. They have no investment in you. And they have nothing to lose by denying you and your needs. While it may appear as inhumane or immoral, others will do what is best for them, and we cannot change that.

When we see something we want, our first impulse is to go after it. But what follows may not be what we are expecting. Placing blame will not change what happened. Consequences are a learning experience that provides foresight into the future.

Consequences raise your awareness to others' needs. They teach you to rely on your intellect rather than emotions when making choices that will alter your life. When someone hurts you, instead of throwing accusations at them, learn why they are hurting you. What do they want that you are not giving them? The pain you are experiencing may be coming from your failure to live up to their expectations.

Failures follow closely behind mistakes. Not getting what you need to survive is a bigger, more devastating failure than not getting what you want. It is not something we want to admit to. It is something we *need* to admit to and take responsibility for.

Consequences alter our entire lives and impact our futures. Changes follow that we have no control over. Failures cannot be turned into successes. If we could eliminate failure, the word would have disappeared from our vocabulary a long time ago.

Consequences are something we can defy in our minds when we foresee them. We cannot defy them by ignoring them when they become a reality. They make it impossible to move forward in life. It can be impossible to change things after a mistake is made. It is easier to make changes in our actions before defying the consequences we foresee in our imaginations.

Choices are made every day, every hour, and every second of our lives. Something follows all of them. Sometimes things change. Sometimes they stay the same. We can gain things, or we can lose things.

Focusing on our needs and responsibilities gives us some stability in our lives. We will always have needs and responsibilities. That will never change.

Your choices affect others. Their choices affect you. It is an unintended consequence that can be unexpected. Failing to learn social responsibilities allows your fears to teach you how to react inhumanely, immorally, and immaturely.

Pride prevents us from accepting failure as an option. Futures are always full of promises that we feel we are deserving of. Disappointment, despair, deprivation, and desperation follow failure. They cause discomforts and vulnerabilities that are difficult to foresee and even harder to escape from. It can become your future. Are you deserving of that?

9

VULNERABILITIES OF UNCONDITIONED INSTINCTS

Do you have maturity? Do you have humanity and morality? Do you have independence? Do you understand their true meanings? Are your answers to those questions right? What happens if you are wrong?

The answers to those questions are coming from your instincts. Instincts cause us to respond, without forethought, to our emotions, people, and experiences. We rely on our instincts for many things. They are essential to the choices we make. If they are not honed and strengthened, we will make bad choices, exposing the vulnerabilities hiding inside of us.

Instincts are mysterious and invisible and easy to neglect. Our knowledge of them can be limited to what we know about fear and the whole flight-or-fight response they trigger. What we may not know is that outcomes are controlled and managed, possibly even manipulated, by our instincts. Knowing that does not mean we can prevent failure as an outcome. It means our instincts can leave us exposed and vulnerable to the events that occur naturally in our everyday lives.

Your instincts need to mature, just like you do. Society has evolved, and we are much smarter than our ancestors were. They focused on developing survival skills and have passed down that knowledge to us. We need to focus on conditioning our survival instincts. Failure is inexcusable, while, at the same time, it is still unavoidable. The world has gotten more competitive, and we need our instincts to guide us through all the challenges that cause us to become combative.

Your instincts can teach you things you did not know about yourself. Who are you? What are you capable of accomplishing in your life? If your success depended on your ability to maintain peace in your relationships, could you rely on your instincts to teach you how to survive? Confronting the fears, insights, consequences, and truths hiding in your mind can teach you how to answer those questions honestly.

Instincts trigger the flight-or-fight response before we even know what we are fighting against or running from. Flight or fight means cooperation or rebellion. It means trust or distrust. It means respect or disrespect. It means building or destroying.

It means fighting with people to get what we want or running from people who can give us what we need. It can take on various meanings that can enable or hinder our survival.

Consequences cause us to feel victimized. It can bring out our combative nature instead of our competitive nature. Being socially responsible is not giving in to the feelings that lead to conflict. Social responsibilities teach you to rise above it so you can remain competitive through adversity. You learn to focus on the solution to your problems rather than fighting over who is to blame for them.

Anger and resentments hide in a combative nature. It destroys the competition through any evil, imaginable and unimaginable. Inhumanity, immorality, immaturity, and dependencies are evils hiding inside of us that can be used to destroy others and their lives. They are sins of neglect.

We are not born with humanity, morality, maturity, or independence. We have a social responsibility to make a conscious choice and effort to learn them. Learning social responsibilities conditions our instincts for survival by teaching us how to foresee threats to our safety and security.

We need humanity, morality, maturity, and independence, not just to succeed but to survive in this forever-changing and competitive world. They provide us with coping and social skills. They transform the anger in us into a will to live.

We can do the wrong thing knowing it is wrong and refuse to do the right thing even when we know it is right. We can be punished for doing the right thing, and rewarded for doing the wrong thing. Life is full of contradictions. All those inconsistencies are what make life challenging.

People are rewarding or punishing. Rewards and punishments create challenges that make us smarter. Society uses them as consequences to tell us when we are right or wrong. Rewards and punishments teach us to nurture our competitive nature while repressing our combative nature. They sharpen and strengthen our survival instincts. Without them, we are weak and vulnerable to our own neglect. Being wrong can trigger events that leave us trapped in fear.

Rewards and punishments condition our beliefs, our emotions, our actions, our hopes, and our expectations. It does not change what we need to survive. Rewards and punishments can override our instincts to do the right thing and cause us to neglect the needs and responsibilities necessary for survival.

Social responsibilities give us control over the choices leading up to rewards and punishments. We rely on our instincts for the choices we do not have time to think about before we need to act. They are dependent on what we *believe* to be true, not necessarily what *is* true. They function to keep us safe and secure. It does not happen if what we believe to be true is false.

VULNERABILITIES OF UNCONDITIONED INSTINCTS

Your instincts cannot keep you safe if you do not listen to them. Ignoring your fears instills a bad habit of ignoring all the threats and risks when you foresee them. Running from all the truths your fears try to teach you will not protect you from reality.

Instincts react to what you foresee in your imagination. Some truths are extremely painful. We can be too scared to confront them when we foresee them. Instead of fighting our way through them, we can run from them by refusing to believe them.

The truth is often mistaken for fear and ignored. Hiding things in the back of our mind is actually instinctive. We see it as self-preservation. Fear is a powerful, intimidating emotion that causes us to feel threatened. Hiding it is our way of running from it. It gives us a sense of control.

Fear makes us think we have something to lose. Running from fears of rejection and failure prevents us from learning the truth about what we have to gain and lose. Conditioning our instincts means training them to tell us when we need self-restraint. We can choose not to fight or run from our fears. We can train ourselves to stop and learn from them.

There are secrets hiding in humanity, morality, maturity, and independence that give you knowledge that empowers you to confront your fears. Learning them gives you an understanding of them and how they keep you safe from yourself and others.

They influence the choices you do not have the time to stop and think about.

Outcomes show you what you do not know and need to know. When the unexpected happens, the beliefs that influenced your choices were wrong. If someone is not who you expected them to be, your beliefs about them were wrong. If you did not get what you wanted from someone, your beliefs were wrong. You cannot change or control who someone is or what they give you. When your beliefs are wrong, your instincts are wrong. It means you made a mistake because of false beliefs.

Just because your instincts are wrong, it does not mean your choices are wrong. At the time you made them, they were what was right for you. Every choice every one of us makes is based on what we want or need.

Being wrong teaches you the truth and gives you knowledge you did not have before making a choice. Outcomes tell you when you are harboring false beliefs and trusting people you cannot trust to give you what you want. Learning from them gives you knowledge you can use to make choices that lead to different outcomes in the future.

Good people do bad things. Good people make mistakes. Good people hurt good people. It is wrong to see only the good in others and expect only good to come out of them. Evil is not something we see in others. It is something we learn about them and ourselves.

Choices are harder to make if you consider the possibility of evil hiding inside of someone. We all have secrets that we do not want others to know. It is a truth that is easy to see as fear and ignore. Your instincts cannot protect you if you do not see others for who they really are.

Your attraction to others begins with what they have to give to you. The truth about anyone can be learned. We can learn to develop our powers of perception to enable us to judge people on sight. We can learn to see the truth without making guesses or assumptions, and without asking questions. We can learn to trust our instincts to prevent others from getting the opportunity to hurt us.

Before you can trust your instincts, you need to trust your beliefs in right and wrong. Otherwise, your instincts will misguide you every time. Unconditioned instincts leave you exposed and vulnerable to all the evils in the world.

Develop a habit of looking for humanity, morality, maturity, and independence in others to keep yourself safe. You do not need to get close to them to see it. You can keep your distance while you decide if they pose a threat to you. It can condition your instincts to look for the truth.

Do they think for themselves? Do they have control over the choices they make, or are they still learning to get control over themselves? If someone has learned right from wrong, you will be able to observe it in them just by looking at them and listening to your instincts.

Passing judgments on others is the right thing to do as long as you hold yourself up to the same standards that you hold everyone else up to. There is nothing wrong with wanting to keep yourself safe. It strengthens your beliefs in right and wrong.

Misunderstandings of our social responsibilities hide in our mistakes. False beliefs are the result of misinterpreting right and wrong. It causes doubts and confusion. There is nothing that can prevent uncertainty. It provides us with the opportunity to train ourselves to question our beliefs instead of starting a battle over right and wrong. Conflict is an outcome that tells us we are wrong about something.

We can be wrong about many things before learning we are wrong about everything. We make choices based on knowledge we have at the time. Learning begins the day we are born. We begin choosing what to believe as true and what is not true at very early ages. We gain the ability to trust our instincts over time when we learn to trust the truth and stop ignoring it.

As humans, we can become so focused on our vulnerabilities that we ignore the truth of what is going on inside of us. The imagination is where our beliefs interact with reality. It is where misinterpretations occur and provoke a fight-or-flight response inside of us. Misinterpretations cause us to fear things we should not fear and not fear the things we should fear. That means we can do a whole lot of running and fighting we do not need to do.

Fear is a natural response based on unconditioned instincts. Actions create realities. Words stimulate imaginations to see realities. Words and actions have meanings that trigger instincts. False beliefs cause us to misinterpret words and actions we fear. It causes us to run when we do not need to and to fight for something that is not going to happen.

> Instincts show us what we believe to be true.

The mind can become a busy, noisy place, making it difficult for us to think. Ignoring it has consequences. Learning social responsibilities quiets the mind so we can focus on our needs. Our needs make us vulnerable. They force us out into the world and into relationships that can scare us.

Thoughts trigger emotions and instincts. Confronting the things that scare us while they are still in our imaginations conditions our instincts and teaches us not to run away from things we need to learn. It is safer to learn through the imagination than by being unprepared for the reality when it happens.

The future is full of unknowns that we learn to see through our instincts. We get clarity through maturity. Knowledge hides in our instincts. Knowledge also controls our instincts. Instincts show us what we believe to be true. False beliefs cause problems we have a responsibility to prevent.

Rewards and punishments can interfere with the maturity process. Inhumanity, immorality, immaturity, and dependencies are a real threat to our lives, our relationships, our safety, and our security. It is more difficult to see in ourselves than in others. It becomes visible in the outcomes of the choices we make.

Conditioning your instincts involves learning how to discriminate between your needs and wants. Unconditioned instincts leave you vulnerable to fear and neglect. Your instincts communicate with you through your fears. Your fears help you define who you are and what you need to survive. Your fears tell you when you are unprepared for the reality you foresee in your imagination.

Success is not measured by your ability to get what you want. It not measured by the number of people who accept you. You are judged by what you are able to accomplish. Your success will be measured by your ability to conquer your fears and insecurities

VULNERABILITIES OF UNCONDITIONED INSTINCTS

to take control over yourself. It is measured by your ability to survive and take responsibility for yourself.

Foreseeing consequences helps you battle your fears of the unknown. Preparing for the consequences you foresee raises your level of confidence in the choices you make. People succeed because they put their needs before their wants. People have authority because they learned to discriminate between responsibilities and neglect. Their instincts earn them their independence.

Confronting your fears does not mean it will lead you to failure any more than ignoring your fears leads to success. Confronting failure can divert you onto a path that is right for you. It can change your goals and plans. It can lead you somewhere you never could have imagined without the help of your fears.

We are told to trust our instincts — not because they are always right, but because they give us insight into our own beliefs. They can feel right and be wrong. They can feel wrong and be right. Trusting our instincts is an opportunity to learn when we are wrong and correct ourselves before we make the same mistakes again.

Society punishes neglect. Society has evolved and developed defenses. It has a collective, or shared, will that protects its values and defends itself against people who threaten its safety and security with nothing more than sins of neglect.

SINS OF NEGLECT

The punishment for neglect is deprivation. Depriving you is not a conscious choice others make. It is what naturally follows when they take responsibility for their safety and security.

Being deprived makes us angry, but it teaches us right from wrong. Ignoring your needs and responsibilities leads to desperation and dysfunction. It is wrong to blame society for it. Being responsible conditions your instincts and teaches you to discriminate against neglect and people who are a threat to your safety and security. Social responsibilities teach you to be protective of yourself and reward others who do the right thing.

Getting what we need to survive is a reward for doing the right thing. Your instincts guide you to making choices that serve someone's wants or needs. Are they satisfying yours? If your choices are rewarding others and leaving you feeling deprived and neglected, your instincts are telling you to reward the wrong people. If your instincts are wrong, you need to train yourself to respond to the truth that your fears are trying to teach you.

Our instincts, guided by false beliefs, lead us straight toward failure. Sin and neglect are punished. Unconditioned instincts leave us vulnerable to the consequences that follow sins and neglect. The punishments are difficult to foresee because we do not see sin as sin. Neglect turns failure into lust, and we misinterpret it as perseverance.

10

INJUSTICES OF DESERTING GOD

What does God expect of us? What does society expect of us? The answer is the same for both God and society. They both expect us to act socially responsible. They both expect us to take control over ourselves regardless of the challenges and obstacles put between us and what we want. They both promise rewards and punishments as incentives.

All of us have some knowledge of God. It is hard to escape. When we think about God, the battle between good and evil tends to follow along with Him. Evil is never far away from our thoughts. Our understanding of God influences our understanding of evil and our choices to fight against it. We look for the good and evil in every choice we make to ensure we make the right choices and trust the right people.

Believing in God is not enough to keep us out of evil's path of destruction. Hiding our fears has blinded us to evil and its path. Evil is difficult to foresee without first seeing the evil hiding in ourselves. Our blindness causes us to become a threat to our own safety, security, and happiness.

Believing in God affects our beliefs and understandings. It affects our actions — especially the ones no one can see us doing. No one can see us thinking or feeling. No one can see us planning or setting goals for ourselves. We can do a lot of things no one can see us doing like God does. We can learn things from God no one knows we are learning.

We can put faith in God and keep it a secret. No one can see us doing it. You could be doing it right now, without even realizing it. Your faith could be buried in habits your ancestors taught a very long time ago.

Everything we learn is stored in our memories. It is a private place in our minds where God likes to hide. The memories we have stored in the back of our minds become knowledge that has power over our instincts. We can see the influence God has over our choices by looking into our minds.

Our knowledge of sin hides inside of our memories, right next to God. When we think about doing the wrong thing, it is easy to push God so far back into our minds that we forget all about Him. When we give sin more power over us than God, we can find God hiding in the consequences.

Faith causes us to have certain expectations of God. There are things we do not do because we believe God is doing it for us. Like fighting evil. Some of us believe it is God's sole responsibility to keep us safe. And it appears as if He is losing the battle.

God cannot fight the war against evil alone. He needs our support. We are either fighting with Him or against Him. Doing the right thing shows our support for God. Doing the wrong thing is desertion. Deserting God causes us to see the bad things that happen as an injustice.

Deserting God causes changes inside of us that we have no control over. It causes us to struggle in life, and no one can see us doing it. It can feel like an injustice. When we do not see others struggling, we feel lost and alone. The pain can be intense.

We put faith in God to end our struggles. We put faith in others and society to end our struggles. It is faith that can hide in our habits, and it can go unrewarded. It can cause doing the wrong thing to appear rewarding.

In our imaginations, deserting God frees us to do things that are defined as wrong. Doing the wrong thing has grave consequences. Deserting God causes us to misinterpret the consequences or punishments as injustices, which can lead to us avenging ourselves. We have a social responsibility to understand the consequences of doing the wrong thing and do whatever is necessary to prevent them.

Learning social responsibilities inspires and motivates us to achieve success and prosperity. It teaches us to set goals and make plans for the future. It teaches us to overcome the challenges and obstacles that humans have control over, not God.

Evil is a reality. We need to learn what it is and how to see it for ourselves. There are grave consequences for ignoring it. God shows us what evil is through our goals and plans for the future. He teaches us how to fight against it through the things we learn confronting our fears.

If we put faith in God to support us when we do the right thing, we need to put faith in God to tell us when we are doing the wrong thing. God is the highest form of authority known to humans. God can see into the past and the future with razor-sharp precision. He foresaw the battle between good and evil. He knew we would fall prey to our own neglect.

Every plan we devise has flaws that leave us vulnerable, and God sees all of them. We have powers of perception to know and understand others. It is not as easy as we think to keep secrets. God hides inside of us, right next to all the good and evil inside of us. He sees everything and knows everything, including our deepest, darkest secrets. And He is not afraid to share them.

Evil is a threat to everyone. That evil hides in every member of society. In the past, our ancestors failed to do the right thing because they did not know what the right thing was anymore. Their neglect is bringing out the evil in us. As a consequence, it has divided society, and it is creating challenges and obstacles that are difficult to foresee.

Our understanding of God affects our understanding of the choices we make and the events that follow. If we have a misunderstanding of God, we fight against good and everything God has done for us. God defined right and wrong a very long time ago. Sin was defined a long time ago. It has been misinterpreted for just as long.

When people betray us or fail to live up to our expectations, it does not just cause unhappiness, it causes us to fail. The effects of it are not as easy to see as the causes of it. Being denied what we want hurts beyond our wildest imaginations, and we have been taught to see it as an injustice. It has created habits hiding inside of us that turn us against each other.

Evil is an enemy we cannot see until after it hurts us. The reason we are blind to evil is because we have developed an expectation of others to give us what we want. As a consequence, our choices are leaving us vulnerable to the evil hiding in others. Our instincts are leading us to unhappiness. Unhappiness has evolved into an evil that demands justice.

God promises to avenge us. There is no proof that God keeps that promise. It is a hard truth to believe in when you are scared and hurting. Faith is all we have, and it is all about believing things we cannot prove.

We can learn humility from God, and no one can see us doing it. It allows us to maintain our innocence. Avenging ourselves has consequences. Believing that is the right thing to do. Revenge shows we have no faith in God.

It is challenging to learn humility because we never know where it is going to lead us. What follows humility? Is it self-control? Is it self-deprivation? Or both?

We can develop mental blocks that make learning difficult when we feel threatened or wronged. It causes us to defy consequences and rebel against authority, even God. There is evil hiding in humanity, morality, maturity, and independence that has been kept a secret for generations. It is a necessary evil inspired by God to protect us against the evils hiding in neglect.

Unhappiness affects our judgments of people we believe wronged us. Injustices are seen as an evil. Sometimes the evil we see in others is not evil. Sometimes, it is God we see in them.

Sometimes our failure is God standing in the way of what we want. It takes humility to see that.

Seeing the failure and unhappiness that follows as an injustice is what is causing the war between good and evil. Unhappiness causes us to redefine right and wrong in the privacy of our own mind. It makes us a threat to our safety and security, along with society's. It causes us to lose faith in God and create dependencies on others to fill the void left by God and our failure.

Deserting God allows us to redefine right and wrong, which causes us to cross boundaries defined by God. It blinds us to our own sins and neglect. When our vision of right and wrong conflicts with God's vision, it puts us at war with God. We see Him as an evil and fight against Him. As a consequence, He deprives us of what we want, leaving us begging for mercy, with nowhere to turn for comfort.

Rejection and failure hurt beyond belief, but it is not the end of the world. People make mistakes by making promises they cannot keep. As painful as it is, it is still just a mistake caused by our own neglect. Our unhappiness over it reveals our need to take responsibility for our safety and security. It shows us where we made a mistake in the past and placed trust in the wrong people.

If you have faith in God, you do not see the rejection or failure or the unhappiness that follows as an injustice. Humility teaches you to empathize with the mistakes others make and their struggles to do the right thing. Morality creates social boundaries that protect us from the devastating effects that unhappiness can have on us.

Some believe God's power is greatly overestimated and even mythological. Our unhappiness proves God's power is real. It is karmic justice for sins of the past. If we are unhappy, it is because we crossed boundaries to get what we wanted. We have a responsibility to learn what boundaries we crossed to get it. Did we cross the boundaries of humanity? Morality? Maturity? Independence? Or perhaps all of them?

> When our fears become a reality, we see them as injustices.

The answers hide in the fears we are too scared to confront. To win the war against evil, all we need are strong beliefs in right and wrong as defenses. Confronting our fears builds them up. Believing in God strengthens them.

Fears can become paralyzing. When that happens, our faith in God is the only thing that can get us through them. It is wrong to put faith in a belief that we can do whatever we want and that God will spare us from the bad things that follow. It leaves us defenseless after we have crossed boundaries.

We put faith in our instincts to teach us right from wrong. So does God. Our instincts have taught us to hide all of our neglect and sins in the back of our minds, where only God can see them. He knows they secretly reveal themselves through the choices we make.

God tests our ability to maintain control over ourselves through fear. Are you ready for it? In what areas of your life do you need self-control? The tests challenge us to achieve our highest potential as human beings.

Your struggles reveal your weaknesses and your fears. God uses our fears to warn us of the evils and threats that follow the choices we make. When our fears become a reality, we see them as injustices. They test our humanity, morality, and maturity. God expects us to react with humility, not rebellious pride. Deserting God causes us to react to God's test with righteous indignation directed at society.

Because of all the unknowns and unexpected events in our lives, we have developed a hidden dependency on God to take responsibility for keeping us safe and secure. It has led us to neglect the responsibility we have to keep ourselves safe. As a consequence, rejection and failure cause us to fear for our safety and security. It causes our distrust of others to consume our imaginations, and we chase after what we want to distract us from it, thinking it will make us happy.

Believing in God, something we cannot see, teaches us how to use our instincts to see the many things we cannot see hiding inside of us and in others. All of the evils and injustices in the world can be traced back to God. Our beliefs in Him have ignited anger that has erupted into wars and battles that never end. The causes of that conflict hide inside our unhappiness.

The past has shown us the threats to our safety and security. It has shown us everything there is to fear and everything we need to fear. It shows us the risks we are willing to take to get what we want. It exposes the path to success and failure so we can learn to see it for ourselves.

In hindsight, we can see how all our fears tried to warn us about various threats. All the injustices tell us we have deserted God. The past has given us foresight to prevent us from making the same mistakes over and over again.

The solution to our problems lies in the prevention of them. If we can foresee mistakes, we can take steps to prevent them. If we can foresee our needs, we can take steps to satisfy them. If we can foresee the threats, we can take steps to protect ourselves. We have the power and the freedom to make choices that lead to us taking responsibility for our safety and security.

Injustices are caused by choices others make of their own free will. They are choices others make that are right for them.

They are choices others hope will lead them to happiness. It is not easy to understand that in hindsight. Confronting our fears of failure and rejection prepares us for it.

Unhappiness causes us to cross boundaries to make life unfair for others. It is difficult to see God in choices others make. Others see Him even if we cannot understand the logic behind their choices. Others will make choices that hurt you. It does not mean they are evil. It just means they are making choices they believe are right for them.

God guides all of us to make choices that are right for us and our individual lives. God gives us hopes that align with His vision of the future. God delegates responsibilities through our faith and hopes. Rewards hide within those responsibilities. So do burdens. Unhappiness causes the responsibilities to become burdensome for us. Unhappiness is not something we can run from like we can responsibilities. It always follows sins of neglect.

God promises us faith, hope, and love. Deserting God changes their meanings in our imaginations. Instead of providing us with the inspiration and guidance we need to succeed, our struggles lead to failure. The faith, hope, and love God gives to us provide us with all the motivation we need when our struggles begin and all the inspiration we need to lead us through the unhappiness that follows.

Social responsibilities hide in faith, hope, and love. We would not be able to function without them. Faith, hope, and love are hiding in every choice we make. And we take them for granted. We just assume they will always lead us to doing the right thing.

We neglect our responsibilities by focusing only on the promises hiding in them. Ignoring others' hopes and expectations is a common mistake that is easy for any one of us to make.

Evils and fears can hide in our beliefs in God. Because of that, God will desert us so we are forced to fight evil on our own, without His support. The pain and unhappiness can last an eternity. It reveals our dependency on God, not our faith in God. He will use what He knows about us to interfere with our lives whenever necessary to break our dependencies on Him and others. It is called Divine Intervention.

Divine Intervention appears as an injustice. God interferes in our lives whether we believe in Him or not. God will wait for you to get what you want and take it all away from you if you neglect your needs and responsibilities.

Divine Intervention is when everything falls apart. Neglect leads to loss and devastation. It tells you when you have no control over yourself or your life. Neglect begins inside of you, and you may feel powerless to stop it. When you choose to ignore your fears, the knowledge you put faith in misleads you.

Neglect prevents anything from happening in your life naturally. You need to work harder and longer to make things happen, and it rarely goes as you expect it to. Neglect teaches you how to manipulate and control your experiences so you can feel happiness. It is not control over your life — it is a loss of control over it. Relationships and experiences should happen naturally.

Punishments teach us humanity, morality, maturity, and independence. Learning them allows good things to happen naturally in our lives, instead of bad things. Social responsibilities put us on the path to the rewards that follow as a result of making the right choices.

There are punishments for deserting God. The path to happiness is not paved with sin and neglect that we can simply shove to the back of our minds and forget. We have a social responsibility to fight against the evil inside of us. Otherwise, our choices will reveal a dark side of God we did not know existed.

11
EMPTY PROMISES OF AVOIDING REALITY

God's existence is not some empty threat to get us to do the right thing. The reality is that we need God's support in our fight against all the evils in the world. The past has shown us what happens without it. We can see all the pain that follows when we make choices that do not result in the outcomes we expect.

We make choices believing we are safe, and when we get hurt, we blame others. Getting hurt means we made a mistake. We need to stop blaming others and make choices that prevent us from repeating our mistakes. We need to start trusting our insights into people and accept the reality that the risks can outweigh the rewards.

Our ancestors were taught that rewards can be misleading and manipulative. They were taught to believe that doing the wrong thing was punished. Reality is validating those teachings.

If we can foresee bad things happening, we need to stop and learn to prevent it. Sometimes the only way we can learn the truth about anything or anyone is through our instincts. We need to learn from the rewards and punishments that follow every choice we make. The choices we make can be based on immaturity. The maturity we gain from learning can teach us how to attract what we want so it exceeds our expectations.

We reward and punish others. They reward and punish us. It is a cycle that has taken us through evolution. To end the pain it causes, we need an understanding of human nature. We need to understand what motivates us to reward or punish someone, and then apply that knowledge to others' choices and behavior.

We are human. That means we are inspired and motivated by our wants and needs rather than our beliefs in right and wrong. We use our beliefs in right and wrong to pass judgments on others. We reward and punish them based on our judgments of them. Being human means we can make mistakes when it comes to our judgments of right and wrong, and of others.

We are usually the last to know when we have made a mistake. The people we hurt are usually the first to know. Your guilt looks different in your imagination than others' guilt does. You see your guilt as a mistake. You see yourself as a victim of others' guilt and something they have control over.

If others have control over the mistakes they make, then so do you. Mistakes are not just choices that deprive us of what we want. They are also choices that deprive others of what they want. You have a responsibility to correct the beliefs leading up to them.

You have a responsibility to correct your beliefs when they are wrong. No one can do it for you. They are your beliefs in your mind, and you have control over them, even if it appears as if you don't.

We choose what to believe and what not to believe. It is a habit we have lost sight of. Punishments are used to make us conscious of it and lead us to making better choices that are rewarding for ourselves and for others.

The future is dependent on every choice we make. When we feel strongly that we are right, that is the time to question it. What will follow if we are wrong? How will it hurt us? What do we have to lose? It is wrong to focus only on what we have to gain when the reality is that we have something to lose also.

Every choice we make changes reality. Choices lead to conflict. They disrupt lives and relationships. We are never alone in the choices we make. Choices impact you and others, and every other choice that follows.

We have developed habits that lead to stability. Our mistakes shatter that stability. They destroy and cause damage that cannot be repaired. People are victimized by mistakes. Even though mistakes are the result of unknowingly doing the wrong thing, people develop fears because of mistakes. Over time, people will begin to fear you if you repeatedly make mistakes.

Mistakes happen when you have no control over yourself. It means your emotions — or something you want — has control over you rather than logic and intellect. Mistakes make us smarter and give us an opportunity to get control over ourselves. It is easy to let those opportunities pass by and keep things the way they are.

Change is hard to do — and even harder to live with. We can do everything wrong and still try to maintain our innocence. In reality, resisting change is how we attempt to hold on to our immaturity. We would rather try to succeed at adapting to our mistakes and living with the pain and suffering than admit to being wrong.

Reality does not lie. It always has a story to tell, and it always tells the truth. We can deny and ignore it all we want. It is not going to change its story. We need to believe that reality is always being honest with us and focus on what follows next. What will happen tomorrow? What will happen next week? A year from now? What will happen after we learn the truth about someone?

If you believed, in the past, that God would keep you safe, and He allowed you to get hurt, what do you need to learn from it? What can you learn from God? What can you learn from the past? What do you need to learn from reality? What other beliefs do you have that are wrong?

Believing God will keep us safe from consequences is a false belief, a fantasy. It is not reality. Our beliefs in God teach us the things we can do to keep ourselves safe. Believing in God keeps us safe from the consequences of disbelief. Morality spares us the consequences of immorality. Nothing can protect us from choices based on false beliefs and the punishments that follow.

False beliefs hide in the choices we make. They hide in the memories stored in the back of our mind. False beliefs lead us to believe that God — or other people — are responsible for giving us everything we want and need. Believing that God — or any person — can fulfill our every hope and dream is a fantasy. All we have to do is look around us, and we can see all the shattered lives to know it is not true.

You can make mistakes, and no one can see you doing it. You can set goals for yourself and never achieve them. You can make plans for the future that never become a reality. Your struggles can lead to failure that is difficult to hide from anyone. Our mistakes have a bad habit of becoming public knowledge without our consent or knowledge.

That is the reality of guilt. It tends to follow choices we make trying to avoid reality. Fantasies make it easy for us to make empty promises and deny hurting others. Others are forced to repair the damage of our mistakes while we continue to make them over and over again.

That is the reality for victims, not their fantasy. No one wants to spend their life cleaning up after someone's mistakes. Ignoring your responsibilities places burdens on others and victimizes them. It can put pressure on them to punish you. Punishments are difficult to foresee when you choose to avoid reality and allow fantasies to dominate your imagination.

Reality hurts. We foresee our fear of it and run straight into our fantasies. We hide ourselves in our fantasies, and no one can see us doing it until we start neglecting our needs and ignoring our responsibilities.

Our ancestors taught us to give in to our emotions and dreams, and we learned at the expense of our survival. Fantasies create a habit of putting faith in false hopes and seeing it as faith in God. Fantasies redefine faith, hope, and love in our imaginations. They take responsibilities off of us and put the burden on others.

Our expectations of life have changed over time. They have become inflated and unrealistic. It is wrong to make choices based on the rewards that we imagine are waiting for us while, at the same time, completely ignoring all the responsibilities and needs we have that are demanding our attention.

We develop attractions to rewards. We nurture them with our persistence and tenacity. Life is not going to give us anything more or different than it gave to us in the past. Our ancestors have survived fear and unhappiness for generations. So can we.

Our ancestors went through the same fears and overcame the same challenges as we are facing today. Fears bring up multitudes of doubts and uncertainties. It can be paralyzing and lead to neglect. Faith in God got them through it. Proof of that is in the past. They managed to live and tell about it.

> Confronting our fears prepares us for reality.

They also had the same hopes we have. Hopes make promises for our safety and security. If our hopes are based on false beliefs, those hopes are not real. If our hopes are not real, the promises are empty. We are neither safe nor secure. False beliefs put us at risk.

Our beliefs in God reveal the responsibilities we have for ourselves. If we believe God will keep us safe and secure, we need to use His teachings to keep ourselves safe and secure. If we believe God will fulfill our dreams, we need to take the necessary steps to fulfill our own dreams. That means encounters with all kinds of people and experiences that may leave us more traumatized than fulfilled.

False beliefs alter our understanding of reality. Fear can fuel our hopes. The more scared we get, the stronger our hopes get. Desperation is an evil that hides in our hopes. It is caused by the needs and responsibilities we neglect. It causes failure and rejection to shatter our lives and our self-esteem.

Self-esteem comes from being right. Beliefs need to be based on truth that reality validates. Truth hides in reality. Empty promises hide in fantasies. We have developed a habit of avoiding reality and denying the truth that is clearly visible in it. The imagination is infamous for creating fantasies motivated by fears we are too scared to confront. It blinds us to reality.

Empty promises or fantasies are like bubbles. They burst and shatter our happiness, taking our self-esteem down with them. They are filled with false beliefs and high expectations that hide our fear of reality. Reality can shatter every hope and dream we ever have.

For generations, reality has been known for failing to live up to our expectations. We cannot change that through fantasies and empty promises. We have a responsibility to acquire social skills to cope with our disappointments. Self-control teaches us how to cope and adapt to reality using the knowledge we learn through our fears.

Our fears do not have the power to shatter our hopes and dreams like reality does. Confronting our fears prepares us for reality. Confronting them is as simple as not ignoring them. It teaches us to be prepared for anything and everything.

Fear is an emotion. The things we fear are a reality. They hide in our fantasies. They inspire us to make choices based on the rewards and to avoid seeing all the evils hiding in the world. Our needs and responsibilities hide in those evils. We need to choose to prevent our fantasies from blinding us from everything hiding in reality and from a future that is difficult to foresee.

Fear acts as a counter-agent to evil and sin. It warns us about neglect. Its function is to get us to stop and think about the reality that will follow the choices we make. Fears represent real threats to our lives. They foretell of real evils in the world. Avoiding them prevents us from assessing the real risks hiding in every choice we make.

We do not always see the fear hiding in us. We see the courage it provokes in us. Fear hides in courage. We need courage to confront reality and accept it for what it is. It is wrong to use courage to fight for what we want when it is based on a fantasy full of empty promises. The evil inside of us can make us feel powerful. The sin hiding inside of us can make us feel invincible. Feelings of power and invincibility cause us to see the empty promises as a reality.

Our guilt stays hidden in the back of our minds, buried beneath all that courage and hope that inspired our choices in the past. Evil hides in courage just like it hides in everything else. All those rewards you envision do not exist in real life. The rewards you want are not rewards for being a good person. They are privileges with responsibilities hiding in them. Those responsibilities satisfy our needs and the needs of society.

It is wrong to build a life on faith that we put in empty promises or things we want by believing they will make us happy. Fear alters our perception of need. That means we can believe we need something or someone we do not need. We can want something we will not want in the future or after we get it. It is a reality that proves how we are all vulnerable to the manipulations of false beliefs and empty promises.

False beliefs are lies we tell to ourselves to avoid reality. They lead to empty promises. What we want may not make us happy at all. Empty promises can lead to choices that lead to unhappiness. They cause you to feel victimized. They can lead to anger and an intense need for revenge that is not a need at all. Revenge is a want. It is wanting to hurt someone, badly.

Reality proves to us, over and over again, that there are things in life that we have no control over. There are things happening in life that we cannot even see. Things happen every day that affect our lives and put our safety and security at risk. Choices, even injustices, change our lives in unforeseen ways.

Avoiding reality causes us to put faith in false beliefs rather than in God. The truth about everything and everyone hides in reality. We ignore it when it is too painful to confront. Avoiding it will not change it. Denying the truth causes us to put faith in false beliefs because, at the time, we believe them to be true. Avoiding reality and all the truth hiding in it causes all the rewards that we foresee in our imaginations to be nothing more than empty promises.

Reality will interfere with our plans. It will interfere with our lives. It will interfere in our relationships. It will shatter our fantasies. It will expose our false beliefs in just about everything. Reality exposes our neglect. Neglect is an evil that deprives society of what it needs to thrive and prosper.

Fantasies are real. The realities they depict in our imaginations are not real. Fantasies separate the good from the bad. We see the bad as wrong and the good as right. We focus on the good and ignore the bad as if God would never let it happen to us. It causes us to see rejection and failure as an injustice and a punishable offense rather than as an outcome that teaches right from wrong.

Reality tells us, over and over again, that failure and rejection are real. Confronting your fear of it prepares you for it. What will you do if you fail or are rejected? They are realities that cannot be changed, controlled, or manipulated through rewards and punishments.

Having control over ourselves means making choices based on truth and reality. It would be a mistake to ignore what we know to be true even if it scares us or forces us to deprive ourselves of what we want. If you lose control and become a threat to society's safety, security, or independence, God cannot keep you safe.

Bad things that happen are God's way of correcting mistakes made in the past. Bad things expose bad choices made in the past. Reality is telling us that all the threats, risks, and consequences are not going to go away. It is how society maintains order, and God supports it. Society has needs that can be seen in reality. God watches over us to see that we are respecting those needs.

Success requires real knowledge, real skills, and real opportunities. Not everyone gets what they need to succeed. Not everyone has the same experiences that lead to real knowledge, skills, or opportunities. That is why it is important to learn to expect failure, rejection, unhappiness, and disappointment. Stop avoiding reality, and learn to expect the unexpected.

The imagination can play tricks on us. That is why we need the truth. If we cannot accept the truth, reality will hurt. There will be no end to the misery that reality can cause. Avoidance does not make reality disappear. Denial does not make the truth any less true. Confronting reality and truth allows you to make choices that lead to a life that exceeds the expectations of your fantasies.

You need to support and cooperate with society to succeed. The threats to our success are real. Enemies are real. Competition is real. Opponents are real. Sometimes they succeed at causing us to fail, and they will do it based on their beliefs, or disbelief, in God. Reality is teaching us we need beliefs in God to get us through it and to help us survive all the pain it causes.

12

INSECURITIES OF ABANDONING YOUR SOUL

Are you someone who believes in God? Or are you someone who does not believe in God? It affects not only the way others see you, but it also it affects the way you see them and reality. Our judgments are affected by our beliefs, or disbelief, in God.

Our ancestors were taught to judge others' souls as good or evil based on their beliefs in God. That habit has survived evolution, with minor adjustments. We still judge others as good or evil, but our beliefs in God play a smaller role in it. Now, our accomplishments play a dominant role in our judgments.

Judging others is not a habit we can break. It teaches us to see ourselves as God sees us. God passes judgments on us through others' judgments. It is important for us to understand right and wrong to avoid misjudging them and ourselves. Judgments have the power to destroy all of us.

We are all humans. Do we really know what that means? What do we know about ourselves? What do we know about our souls? How does that knowledge affect our judgments?

Many of us focus on the vulnerabilities that come with being human. We use it to justify our actions or excuse us from our wrongdoings. Our insecurities are only part of what it means to be human. There is also a part of us that has the power to conquer our insecurities that is easy to ignore. Failing to exert control over ourselves blinds us to our souls and who we really are.

When we want something, we all have power that feels like it is coming from our souls. It gives us strength and makes us feel as if we are making the right choices. It allows us to believe we are in control — until we get hurt or are wronged by someone we trusted.

We tend to acknowledge our souls most when we are hurting and vulnerable. We feel the pain of neglect deep down in our souls. With everything going on in our lives, it is easy to ignore. Unhappiness causes us to feel lost and alone. It means we abandoned our souls when we needed them the most, before we got hurt.

Abandoning your soul is the same as abandoning yourself. It causes you to turn to fantasies for comfort. Fantasies nourish our souls. It is part of being human. The thought of getting what we want is comforting. What we need to realize is that fantasies are a starting point for our life. Acting on them reveals immaturity and a lack of control over ourselves. It can lead to rejection and failure before we are prepared for it.

It takes more than courage to get what we want. We need an understanding of the power hiding inside of us and in every choice we make. We need knowledge of how fantasies influence the way we see ourselves and others. Reality is not always as it appears in our imagination.

The mature thing to do is keep your fantasies locked away in the back of your mind until you have learned to distinguish between reality and fantasy. Our understanding of human behavior cannot be simplified by classifying our actions as right or wrong. We need an understanding of the needs and desires motivating us before we make choices that fail to give us what we want.

Fantasies are full of false beliefs that cause us to misplace blame and anger when things do not go as we expected. They have the power to cause us to believe that success is guaranteed. Reality is teaching us to believe differently.

Once something has happened, it is too late to prevent it. And it cannot be kept a secret. Fantasies cannot hide what has already become a reality. Avoiding reality causes unhappiness that goes far deeper than being deprived of what you want.

Disappointment leads to a bad habit of disrespecting others and their needs. Disrespect leads to a bad habit of distrusting people, even good people. It is the path to rejection. If your emotions are traveling that path, you are rejecting someone. It all begins when reality fails to live up to our expectations.

Disappointment, disrespect, and distrust are things you can see inside of you before others can. They happen before failure as a result of your rejection of them. They cause you to fear for your safety and security. They can teach you how to take control over others. You have a responsibility to see them as warnings telling you when you need to take control over yourself and your life.

> Insecurities are your personal fears.

Your expectations are also something you can see in your imagination before anyone else can. Your needs hide in them. You need to fear the disrespect and distrust inside of you before others start to fear and distrust you. Disrespect and distrust can prevent you from getting what you want. Fearing them will give you control over them.

Disappointment, disrespect, and distrust are evils and a reality; they become obstacles that sabotage your plans for the future. They happen before mistakes are made. Ignoring the evils hiding inside of you means ignoring your safety and security.

We have lost sight of evil because we no longer fear it. We stop fearing it by believing God will remove all the obstacles in our path for us. We can fail to see the neglect or evil hiding in our habits as a cause of our failure and rejection.

It is wrong to expect God to do the things we have a responsibility to do for ourselves. If we do not learn how to see the obstacles in our path, we cannot learn how to overcome them. The evil hiding inside of us can prevent us from seeing them, and it can lead to insecurities.

You need to be certain you are making the right choices for you. Before you can do that, you need to know who you are. It is not enough to be a good person. People will still hurt you. People will still lie to you. That is a reality you need to be prepared for.

All the evils in the world can draw our attention to what is hiding inside of others. Confronting reality allows us to use our fantasies as an opportunity to focus our attention on what is going on inside of us, not others. What secrets are hiding inside of you?

Emotions. Judgments. False beliefs. Truths. Guilt. Sin. Anger. Unhappiness. Fears. Insecurities. There are so many things hiding in us and influencing every choice we make. They are realities we avoid to get what we want. They are realities we need to get control over. They are realities that show you who you are.

You are hiding inside of you. Your soul is something that hides inside of you, and it communicates with you through everything that happens inside of you. Ignoring it causes you to abandon your soul. It causes you to lose yourself and leads to insecurities that allow you to see yourself as good without any real proof of it.

The good we see in our own souls is our own immaturity. Seeing ourselves as good blinds us to our need for self-control. It closes our minds to learning social skills. It allows us to deny the evil hiding in ourselves, waiting to come out when we believe we have been wronged.

People who give you what you want have power over you. What happens when they do not give you what you want, or stop giving you what you want? Can you survive without them? Can you cope with the loss? Can you walk away from the relationship peacefully? If not, you are making choices that can leave you victimized.

Believing something to be true gives us as much power over our choices as the truth does. However, it leads to different outcomes. The truth will lead you in a different direction than false beliefs will.

We have the knowledge and, therefore, the power to predict outcomes. False beliefs cause us to be wrong. Misjudging ourselves and others has the power to mislead us to unknown, unexpected, and unforeseeable outcomes that are extremely disappointing and painful.

When we want something, we do not stop to think that we need control over ourselves. Desire and attraction are strong emotions that cause us to lose control over ourselves. They have the power to pull our attention away from what is going on inside of us and cause us to ignore everything in their path and everything leading up to our choices. Our choices have the power to define our social identities and our futures. Desire and attraction have the power to take it all away from us.

Fantasies inspire us to be who we want to be rather than to be who we are. It is how we abandon our souls. Abandoning our souls leads to insecurities, not the feeling of it, the reality of it. Without our souls, we wander off from society and go through life alone. We get lost and may never find our way back.

Insecurities are your personal fears. They are full of doubts and uncertainties that cause you to believe others are not doing enough to give you what you want to validate the good in you. It is a false belief that causes you to feel deprived and neglected. Ignoring your fears keeps you connected to them and weakens your will to do what is right for you.

A fear of rejection causes us to seek validation from others. Insecurities cannot be conquered with acceptance. They are overcome by doing what is right for society and for ourselves. Our fears can prevent us from doing the right thing when we believe it is wrong. It does not mean it is wrong. It means we *believe* it is wrong. It is a belief influenced by our fantasies.

Fantasies influence our judgments of right and wrong. They make it difficult to distinguish between lies and truth. Others see who we are through our actions and the choices we make. Our choices can be wrong. We can make choices based on lies we tell ourselves and lies others tell us. It can be based on lies told by generations that are long deceased.

What matters now is that we learn the truth and move forward with it. Fantasies do not show us what happened in the past that can prevent us from getting what we want. They show us the future if we are successful in judging ourselves and others correctly. Focusing only on success hides our fear of failure. It leads to a determination to get what we want, despite what has already happened.

Determination is not a good thing when we are doing something that is wrong for us or leads to neglect. It prevents us from seeing other options in life. Determination causes us to get stuck in one place, on one path in life. It can be an evil that causes us to destroy everything and everyone standing in our way, even other options.

Options have the power to keep hope alive in your soul and prevent you from getting lost in your insecurities. When you abandon hope, you abandon your soul. As humans, we are told the right thing to do is to believe in God and the hope He gives us. It prevents us from getting lost in our own mistakes.

It is difficult to believe in God when we cannot see Him. It is difficult to believe in anything we cannot see. There are many things we cannot see without believing. Believing can help us exert control over ourselves and build up our confidence.

Believing in God influences the way we see ourselves and others. We see our souls as the part of us that harbors the good in us. We see the good in us when we see the evil hiding in others. If we can see the evil in others' souls, it is because others have already seen it hiding in us.

We can see immaturity and irresponsibility in others. We can see those who have no control over themselves. Neglect is visible. If we can see it in others, they can see it in us. That is enough for us to defend and protect ourselves against them. Others' lack of control over themselves should influence the choices we make and prevent us from giving them the opportunity to disappoint us.

The path to unhappiness in your relationships begins with your judgments of the people who hurt you. You can misjudge their ability to give you what you want. It is easier for you to change your judgments of them than it is to change those who hurt you.

Your power and your control hides in the choices you make. Judgments do not have the power to change people into who you want them to be. Judgments have power over you. Use your judgments of them to learn who you are and make changes inside of you.

Changing what happens inside of you is a complicated process that affects every aspect of your life. It takes time to fully accept new beliefs as truth. Changing your judgment of someone changes your future. It causes changes you need to prepare for.

Waiting for others to change causes us to hide our neglect and sins in the back of our minds. A fear of change surrounds our guilt, making it too painful to confront. Unhappiness hides in our souls and expresses itself through our conscience. Ignoring it fuels our fears and insecurities. The time we spend waiting for others to change is time we spend depriving ourselves of what we want.

Learn to listen to yourself, and stay connected to your soul. Your reactions to others can cause fears to surface. What are they saying to you about your needs?

Your needs and habits can tell a lot about you. They begin inside your soul. Things you want come from your soul. Your habits are leading you toward it, and it can reveal your true social identity.

Learning social responsibilities teaches us how to attract people who accept us for who we are, not who we want to be, or who they want us to be. It teaches us to see our need for maturity and morality in relationships so we can cope with failure and rejection.

Feeling deprived and neglected means we need our independence. Admitting we have a need for our independence is difficult. It usually means ending a relationship. It usually means making significant, life-altering changes. It means making major sacrifices.

Many people avoid making changes because they believe that God has the power to change people. It is wrong to believe that God has the power to change people into who you want them to be. It is wrong to believe that rewards and punishments change people into who you want them to be. No one, not even God, can force anyone to do something they do not want to do or cannot do of their own free will.

Rewards and punishments will not change our feelings. Unhappiness is a reaction to an outcome that cannot be controlled or manipulated rather than the result of being victimized. It will not change despite our efforts to change it or others. If we want an outcome to change, we need to change ourselves rather than defend our innocence. Unhappiness is an evil that inspires change.

Unhappiness is an evil that is caused by disappointment. We can blame it on others. While it appears as if they have control over it, they do not have the ability to change your emotions. Others do not have control over your reactions to something they did or did not do.

The right thing to do in life is to build your life on what you have — not on what you want. Learn who you are. Learn your strengths and weaknesses. It will show you what you need to build the life you want. Your needs are specific to you, and they are different from everyone else's needs. Develop habits that satisfy your needs. It will define your path to your independence.

Independence has the power to validate our identity and the choices we make for ourselves. Others see the good in us when we restrain the evil in us. If we want society's acceptance, we need to be concerned with God's judgments of us. God can see into our souls. He works with our souls to determine the course of our life. Our safety and security is His priority. It needs to be ours, too.

Independence is about doing the right thing of your own free will. The outcomes that follow validate God's existence and His support in our lives. Our struggles do not end when we find happiness. Those things we struggle with are responsibilities. They do not always make us happy. They do, however, provide for our safety and security.

We need to take control over ourselves and act against our will when we know it is the humane, moral, or mature thing to do. Our will, like our instincts, can become conditioned to act on what we want. We can condition them to act on our needs by creating a habit of acting on our needs. There are things we need to do even when we do not want to.

Choices are based on beliefs. Beliefs are based on knowledge. Knowledge of what you want and need hides inside of you. Knowledge of who you are hides in your memories, in your actions, in your choices, in your judgments, in your beliefs, and in your needs. It hides in your past and in your future. It hides in your soul.

Staying connected to your soul and to God changes the meaning of happiness. Your soul is the part of you that knows what you are doing wrong. Your conscience is your soul. It knows what you are neglecting. It knows your guilt, and it knows your past. Your soul knows who you are. Ignoring it is ignoring what you do wrong.

Religion has been preaching for generations that sin and neglect are dark stains on our souls. They forever alter the way people see us. They can never be removed from our past or from who we are. They permanently alter our identities and our lives in ways that are difficult to foresee. You cannot see the damage they cause until it is too late.

Maintaining our innocence and independence is a reflection of our soul's character. Confronting our sins and guilt builds character and keeps us connected to our soul and to God. Making changes in ourselves is a reflection of our strength and morality. Independence says something about our character. It is something society can see.

Insecurities hide our true power, as humans, inside of us. Learning social responsibilities reveals the true power hiding in our souls. Humanity, morality, maturity, and independence are social skills that enable our survival. God protects us, as a society, through the social boundaries that our social skills create. Some see these boundaries as "The Divide."

13

CASUALTIES OF RUNNING FROM YOUR BATTLES

What are the casualties of not fighting your battles? That is like asking, "What happens when you do bad things?" The answer is the same for both questions. Casualties are deaths and losses that lead to grief and despair and leave us feeling victimized. There are casualties with any battle that is fought. There are also casualties of battles not fought.

Humanity is a battle against inhumanity. Morality is a battle against immorality. Maturity is a battle against immaturity. And independence is a battle against dependency. They are your battles.

Those are the battles that begin in your imagination. Those are battles you have an individual responsibility to fight. Those are the battles you have control over. Those are the battles that come before the battles that cause The Divide.

Running from those battles causes casualties that divide society. Neglect kills. Relationships die. Trust and respect fade. Souls become tormented. Futures cease to exist. People become victims. Those are the things we can see happening as a result of The Divide. What about the things we cannot see?

All kinds of bad behaviors have been tolerated for generations while we try to learn ways to manipulate events and others to get what we want. It is difficult to see the loss of our character and integrity that follows as a result. It is even more difficult to see what follows that.

Fighting against sin and neglect is how we learn social responsibilities. The battles you fight inside of you should lead to you cooperating with others. It gives you dignity, along with clarity of human nature.

Social responsibilities define a path to peace and order. We get lost in conflict and cannot see what we are really fighting over when we fail to discriminate between right and wrong. Doing the wrong thing causes us to fight over things we have no control over.

Manipulations are an attempt to change things we have no control over. It is wrong, and it leads to battles that never end. The Divide is a battle that never ends. Some battles are pointless. Why fight something that has no resolution?

Fighting will not end the divide between wealth and poverty. It will not change the color of our skin, our genders, our religious views, or others. It is like trying to control the weather. There is no reason to be fighting for control over it. It will not change what we want and need for our survival. Fighting over things we have no control over leads to power struggles or karmic battles.

The Divide is full of various karmic battles that are the result of bad things that happened in the past. We are fighting over things we have no control over. The Divide is real. The battles we are fighting are real. They show us how far we have gotten through evolution, or rather how far we have not gotten.

> **Karmic battles force us to fight for control over our lives.**

Our battles with each other reveal our inability to communicate with each other effectively. You can find judgments, even discrimination, in the choices people make. However, you can also find their beliefs in right and wrong, along with their needs and wants. Fighting over it reveals a lack of respect for others and their needs.

Society has become divided by choices each individual makes of their own free will that lead to either neglect or responsibility. Those choices are influenced by our beliefs, by our wants, and by our needs. Conflict will not change any of that. Knowing what we want and need gives us authority over our own lives.

Karmic battles force us to fight for control over our lives. It leads to uncertainty that is not easy to conquer. It interferes with our ability to feel safe and secure. Power struggles force us to fight for our own independence.

Learning to ask for what we need rather than what we want gives us control over our lives by teaching us how to get control over the things we can control, beginning with ourselves and the choices we make to maintain our independence. Our need for independence causes power struggles inside of us. It causes battles over right and wrong that play out in our imaginations.

When we get conflicted over right and wrong, our desires usually win out over our needs. Ignoring our needs and responsibilities is neglect. It is something we have control over. It is something we can change about ourselves.

Fighting our battles with the sin and evil hiding inside of us prepares us for adversity. Running from them is disrespectful to society and its needs. The Divide reveals all the inequalities and injustices causing casualties in life as a result of all the running we are doing. Instead of inspiring us to change ourselves, The Divide is inspiring us to fight for change in others.

It does not take courage to fight a battle. It takes desire or attraction to fight a battle. The things we want give us courage. Fighting for what you want does not change people or the outcomes. It is the beginning of a battle that never ends.

Conflict hides in courage. Courage teaches us how to fight for what we want. Fighting with others prevents us from learning how to ask for what we need and respecting the choices others make. It requires a different kind of courage to walk away from what you want and not fight with others over it. That kind of courage leads to a different outcome. It maintains peace and order.

Adversity does not just cause battles with others. It also causes battles inside of us that prepare us for competition. We need to fight against the effects of adversity that cause us to become aggressive and impulsive. Competition can bring it on in us. It is easy to mistake aggression for courage.

What is competition doing inside of you? Competition is about pushing yourself to succeed, not about fighting with others. Conflict has an effect on us that is easy to ignore. Just because we have the right to go after what we want, is it right to start a war to get it?

Fighting for what we want is how the whole battle between good and evil began many, many, many years ago. The Divide is inspiring us to fight for changes that will punish one side of The Divide and reward the other. Change is not always as rewarding as it appears in our imaginations. It can be punishing when we are not prepared for the responsibilities that follow.

Battles are a form of communication. They are a way of communicating our wants and needs to others. Things we want and need can cause conflict that triggers a flight-or-fight response in us. It is a time to listen and learn so we can fight the battles raging inside of us.

We can fight with each other and lose sight of what happens next. What follows the battles we think we won? What happens when we lose? At the time, all we can see clearly is what we have to gain and lose. Everything that happened before and after becomes distorted in our imaginations.

There are a lot of things that happen that we cannot see clearly, or distortedly. We learn things before and after conflict. We learn about lies, deceit, and betrayals. We learn truths that allow us to see reality more clearly. We learn to clear up misunderstandings and misinterpretations that are happening in our own imaginations.

Conflict gives us clarity on the past and the future. It shows us how vulnerable and easily deceived we all are. It reveals our wants and needs, and what we are not getting. It shows us what we know, what we do not know, and what we need to know. It provides us with knowledge that makes us smarter.

There are things we can learn from past conflicts to prevent them in the future. The past teaches us through hindsight how to prevent conflict in the future through foresight. If we can foresee conflict, we can learn to overcome our impulsiveness to prevent it.

Impulsiveness leads to battles we can run from in the future. We learn things about people later that scare us or make us angry. Relationships that begin with excitement and hopes for the future end in pain and battles over the past.

Conflict teaches us how to keep secrets. We have learned to keep secrets, believing it is a way to prevent conflict and get what we want. What we do not see is that secrets cause changes to reality. They lead to unexpected and unknown outcomes that change the future in ways we cannot foresee or prevent.

Secrets hide things we have no control over. The time we spend learning what people are hiding is time that is better spent on things we have control over. We have battles to fight that can make a real difference in our lives.

Secrets hide sin and neglect that rob us of our independence and ability to take control over ourselves and our lives. People cannot keep secrets forever. Sin and neglect have a way of revealing themselves all on their own.

People cannot hide their inhumanity, immorality, immaturity, and dependencies, no matter how hard they try to. Anyone can see them. It just takes self-control and courage to stop avoiding the reality that sin and neglect create.

Self-control is the only weapon we have to fight against all the evils hiding inside of us. We need to control the things we can if we want to change the outcomes we have no control over. The Divide brings out fears for your safety and security that cannot be conquered with change. They are overcome by learning from the past. How did we get to where we are today? How has society prospered over decades and throughout evolution?

We face competition with the things we want and the things we need. We feel more confident going after the things we want. Things we need can bring out insecurities. It is the reason we put our wants as a priority over our needs. Insecurities are what cause the battles playing out in our imaginations between our wants and needs. Your life becomes a casualty when you run from that battle.

We need to fight against the evils inside of us, not in others. Ignoring the evils hiding in us causes us to turn competition into a battle with others. The battles you think you win with others may never be over. People will fight back when they believe they have been wronged.

Society will judge you on your accomplishments. Learning humanity, morality, maturity, and independence is an accomplishment that reveals the good in you. Others see your soul through them. They see the evil hiding in you when you run from them.

Accomplishments prove our ability to get control over ourselves. They require commitments that teach us how to avoid distractions. Success and stability are built on accomplishments. They are something no one can take away from you, and they give you self-esteem.

Fighting karmic battles leads to feelings of hopelessness. Fighting with each other, regardless of how good our intentions are, will not change what is going on in life. There are battles you need to learn to ignore. Otherwise, they will become a distraction that prevents you from learning what you need to learn for your own survival.

The human race has a past. It is filled with violence and bloodshed. Our beliefs in right and wrong have caused us to kill and destroy just to get what we want. The lesson of forgiveness has gotten lost in all the karmic battles playing out with evolution.

Life has rules. Society has rules. People have rules. Rules define right and wrong. Rules can seem unfair and cause pain we never imagined. It is wrong to allow that pain to dictate what is right and wrong for others or society. Changing the rules will not change the outcomes of choices we make.

Not following the rules in life will cause you to fear for your safety and security, indefinitely. Fear will become a battle that never ends, and it will cause conflict in your relationships. Rules keep people safe. They also create boundaries that prevent us from getting what we want. They trigger rebellious impulses that do not leave us with time to think about the consequences or the effects they will have on our future.

The battles we need to fight are against our impulsiveness and the pain it causes. God and society help us fight against sin and neglect. All we have to do is learn right from wrong. Learning is a battle we fight in our minds or imaginations. It is challenging when you think you are right or that there is nothing to learn. Conflict tells us there is something to learn. It exposes the false beliefs hiding in us.

There are challenges to fighting against beliefs that are wrong. False beliefs are yet another battle we need to fight. The rewards we see on the other side of The Divide are not immediate or foreseeable. They hide in humanity, morality, maturity, and independence. Winning our battles with sin and neglect puts us on the other side of The Divide and gives us clarity.

We need to fight to maintain peace and order that is already established. We need to fight against all the evils and fears hiding inside of us that provoke us to act impulsively. We need to restrain ourselves from trying to control others and the choices they make in an attempt to manipulate an outcome to get what we want.

Conflict becomes a predictable pattern of behavior in our relationships. We are human. It is in our nature to keep secrets and to manipulate the events in our lives leading up to what we want. It is human nature that needs to be controlled to prevent conflict that leads to power struggles with others.

Bad things will follow our attempts to manipulate others and their lives. Manipulations do not change anything. Human nature does not change. It needs to be controlled and managed so we do not get out of control.

Human nature raises many questions we have on our so-called journey through life that test our intelligence of ourselves and others. It questions our knowledge of right and wrong, and of success and failure. The answers to all our unanswered questions hide in the reasons we have been fighting all these battles for so many generations.

If you take the time to stop and think about it, the reasoning behind conflict is simple. We are humans, we have needs, and resources are limited. Competition reveals the sin hiding in us. When things do not go as we expected, we react instinctively with sloth, envy, gluttony, wrath, pride, greed, and lust when we run from our battles against them.

There are lessons we can learn from all the fighting we did in the past. Our ability to survive is dependent on our intelligence and our ability to avoid or prevent conflict with others. It is difficult to do when it goes against everything we believe is right.

As humans, we battle with right and wrong in our minds all the time. It is a constant struggle that never ends, regardless of how much time has passed. Breaking rules and running from your battles will not get you what you want faster.

Life follows a pattern that evolves with society's needs and expectations. Fighting against life will cause casualties. Running from the battles raging inside of you causes you to lose out on what life has to give you.

Life is not ours for the taking. It is wrong to believe we can dominate it, take control of it, and guide it in any direction we want to. The things we cannot control force us to learn how to adapt and cope with reality. Life is a living, breathing force that will fight back.

Life is ours for living. It demands our respect. There is no reason to fight with anyone to get what we want. The past is showing us that The Divide cannot be bridged or conquered with rewards and punishments. Crossing boundaries puts our lives at risk. The Divide was formed, naturally, to keep ourselves safe from the other side and to give us the freedom to follow our own individual paths in life.

There is no doubt that The Divide is unfair. Neither side is happy. Both sides blame the other side. Both sides feel deprived and neglected. Both sides fear for their safety and security. Both sides feel wrongly judged. The reality is that both sides have made mistakes that are a visible part of our past that can no longer be kept a secret.

> It is not easy to prevent ourselves from doing the wrong thing.

When competition or adversity causes us to feel combative or angry, we can get control over ourselves by learning respect for rules. Respect right and wrong when you cannot respect people. Respect their judgements of you. If they are wrong, prove them wrong. Do not make the mistake of starting a battle over someone's judgments of you. It will never end.

When someone passes judgments on you, they are being honest about what they want and need. Fighting with them will not change their judgments of you. It will prove them right about you. Keeping a battle alive out of some misguided need to be right brings out the evil in you.

Goals create a path for us in life. When life seems unfair, follow your goals, and respect the rules. The choices you make along the way create a life for you. Your focus should not be on getting what you want. It should be on your needs and responsibilities.

It is your life. You need to own it and take responsibility for it. Protect it against your own bad choices and judgments. When you learn to judge the evil in yourself, you learn to judge the good in others differently. You see it more clearly in people who have taken the time and put in the effort to learn responsibility.

The longer we run from our battles of taking control over ourselves, the harder it gets. It is not easy to prevent ourselves from doing the wrong thing. As humans, we get confused easily and fall victim to our own beliefs over right and wrong. It is something we learn to prevent as we mature.

Competition and judgments can bring out insecurities that sabotage your plans for the future. Getting control over them is necessary for your success. Happiness is fragile and easily shattered through conflict. It becomes a casualty when you run from your battles.

Happiness is strengthened by learning social responsibilities. It enhances our communication and social skills. If you fail to win the battle over your insecurities, dysfunction and poverty follow. Your safety and security become casualties.

The battles between good and evil are battles over right and wrong. You have an individual social responsibility to resolve your battles with the good and evil in you. You have sole responsibility for getting control over yourself and doing the right thing, regardless of what others do wrong.

The casualties of running from your battles with self-control are faith, hope, and love. Because of competition, we need options that can be seen only with faith, hope, and love. Competition and failure are a reality that requires us to have a backup plan. It helps us to resist the urges to fight with others over what we want.

Faith, hope, and love are realities that make it possible for us to live a life of prosperity and happiness. Learning how to have faith, hope, and love teaches us how to win the battles against sin and neglect. If you do not fight against them, they will destroy you. You will become a casualty.

We expect good to win the battle over evil, but the reality is that sometimes evil wins, and good becomes a casualty. When we do the wrong thing, evil is rewarded and good is punished. When we see evil win, it is actually God defeating the evil in us.

Society is divided by inhumanity, immaturity, immorality, and dependencies. They are battles that are easy to run from when you want something. There are no winners in the karmic battles they cause, only losers. If you run from your battles, the biggest battle you will ever fight is for your sanity. Inner conflict over right and wrong that is left unresolved turns to insanity.

14

INSANITY OF HIDING THE FUTURE

This chapter brings us to the end of a journey that begins with attraction. Our journey through life begins with the things we want. The path to insanity also begins with the things we want. Attraction is a powerful force that allows us to foresee the future while, at the same time, allows us to believe we are sane and rational.

What happens if we are foreseeing the wrong future? What will happen in the future if we are wrong and it is not what we expected? It is easy to justify what we want and make the choice to go after it. However, it is not so easy to justify the neglect along the way.

There is a difference between justifying your choices and rationalizing them. Rationalizations occur in the imagination and rely on knowledge. Rationalizations are where we use knowledge to separate the truth from the lies and fantasy from reality. It is where we foresee the future while lacking clarity on everything that can happen in the meantime.

Knowledge has power only if it is used correctly. Mistakes happen when we use it incorrectly. Mistakes begin with rationalizations that are based on false beliefs that prevent us from seeing lies and fantasies. We are blinded by the excitement they trigger in us. It causes them to appear more rewarding than the truth and reality.

Our futures begin with excitement over the events we see in our imaginations. As uplifting and affirming as excitement can be to our self-esteem, others do not always share our vision, and it can lead to conflict. That is a future that is often hiding in the back of our minds. The excitement makes it easy to ignore.

Hiding the future in the back of our minds prevents us from rationalizing our choices and getting control over our lives. We ignore the truth and reality because of the fear surrounding them. Putting faith in lies and fantasies creates a reality of confusion and insanity that causes unavoidable stress and anxiety inside of us.

We hide the future when there is something hiding in it that we do not want to confront. It is easy to ignore the future we foresee when it brings out fears for our safety and security. They are fears that hide behind all the activity in our imaginations. We believe that ignoring them is a way to outsmart evil and ensure our success in getting what we want.

Instead, learn what fear does to you. Learning really outsmarts evil and all the problems it causes. Learn how fear affects your choices and behavior. How it triggers impulses, instincts, emotions, and the imagination. How it gets control over you and the choices you make. That is knowledge you need for your future.

Fear causes us to hide things in our minds that provide knowledge, such as truths, neglect, sins, and the past. Our lives are at the other end of all the knowledge and power that flow through our imaginations. Choices do not always lead to what we are expecting. The unexpected can happen. Hiding all that knowledge can drive us crazy.

The future is full of the unknown and the unexpected. It is full of things we can foresee and things we cannot foresee. It is not easy to make sense of our lives when there are things we do not know or cannot control. All rational thoughts can escape us when we want something. We need knowledge of neglect to make rational choices.

This book is filled with 14 chapters that define various forms of neglect to give clarity on a future that is difficult to foresee. It teaches you how to see neglect and what follows it. You may not have seen the future yesterday, but you can see it more clearly today.

The future is never clear. Clarity is acquired or learned. It is not given to us. We need to work for it. We need to survive all the unknowns and unexpecteds that surprise and threaten to traumatize us. It develops and strengthens our ability to foresee the future correctly.

This book should give you clarity on the future you are fighting your way into. Our destinations are not always foreseeable, but the battles we fight can paint a picture in our imaginations. Learning social responsibilities is full of battles that will create a future that is different than the one created by fighting against them.

Are you still fighting battles that were resolved a long time ago, or are you ending battles that began long ago? Are you learning to control the things you can control, or are you learning to manipulate the things you cannot control? Your answers will influence your imagination and your future.

Life has divided society despite our best efforts to unite all of us. We believe we have a need to fight for unity to get what we want. What is on the other side of that divide and conflict that we are so attracted to? What do we believe unity will give to us? What is pulling us away from our responsibilities and the life we already have?

The future is not about unity, justice, or equality. Our futures are not a prize for winning a battle. They are a privilege that comes with responsibilities. Regardless of our beginnings in life, we become adults with a need and a responsibility to get control over ourselves.

People do not give you rewards for growing up. They give you responsibilities. Responsibilities hide in the rewards we are chasing after. The whole point of being able to foresee the future is so we can prepare for them. Responsibilities can become oppressive and burdensome. If we do not prepare for them, we can go crazy, literally.

Sanity is being able to make sense of things. Problems get solved, and questions get answered through rationalizations. Our choices in life are made through rationalizations. We need solutions to our problems to prevent ourselves from going crazy.

Sanity thrives on knowledge. Knowledge is power that feeds the imagination and fuels our motivations. The answers we need for sanity are hiding inside of us and in our souls. There are many secrets that hide in our beliefs and in the habits that get us through the day.

There are meanings in everything we do, every thought we have, and every emotion we experience. Right and wrong are defined by those meanings. Sanity comes from finding meaning in right and wrong and reconciling it with our thoughts, emotions, and experiences. That is what rationalizations are. They lead us to answers.

We need to dig deep down into our souls to find meaning in our fears, our needs, and our responsibilities. Everything we hide in the back of our minds provides us with knowledge that becomes a part of our rationalizations for the future. That knowledge becomes the answers hiding deep down in our soul to give us guidance for making the choices that are right for us. We need to stop ignoring them when it is not what we want to hear.

The future you want and the life you create will be different. Reality is always different from the way you foresee it in your imagination. Those differences can be hard to rationalize. They are caused by everything you ignored in the past — all the fears, all the evils, all the threats, all the risks, all the sins, all the neglect, all the guilt, all the truths, and all the responsibilities.

Reality is affected by lies, truth, honesty, and dishonesty, which can be impossible to foresee. The future is influenced by humanity, morality, maturity, independence, boundaries, instincts, reality, consequences, God, battles, the past, our souls, and you. It is also influenced by neglecting them.

Neglect causes us to ignore our safety and security. It deprives us of knowledge and the ability to rationalize our choices. Neglect leads to needs we cannot satisfy, problems we cannot resolve, fears we cannot conquer, and challenges we cannot overcome. The anxiety and desperation that follows is insanity.

Insanity is what follows when you are focused solely on getting what you want and ignoring everything going on inside of you and around you. Insanity is the outcome, or consequence, of neglecting to get control over yourself and your life. It is a future where nothing makes sense anymore.

The future finds all of us, whether we are prepared for it or not. It finds us whether it is what we want or not. The future is where we learn if we made the right choices or the wrong choices in the past. The future is where our hopes and dreams shatter or where life begins.

No one gets to the future unscathed. Life breaks us and our hopes and dreams up into little pieces that can be impossible to put back together. Being deprived of what you want causes unbearable pain. It hurts in ways that are difficult to foresee. Do not fall into the trap of believing that revenge or justice will make you feel whole again or bring about equality.

Over time, our battles for justice and equality have only widened The Divide. Ignoring our social responsibilities has deepened it. We neglect our needs and responsibilities when we have hopes of change. It helps us cope with whatever is happening in the present.

Change does not always unite us. Sometimes it divides us even further. The evil hiding inside a divided society has caused hidden changes inside of us that cause us to be combative. Those changes unexpectedly redefine boundaries for all of us, and we learn to see them through the conflict that arises in our relationships.

Conflict gives us knowledge of human behavior. It does not mean we can change any of it. People get scared and angry. They want things you cannot give them. Things happen for reasons you cannot understand. It creates boundaries we need to learn to see and respect.

> **Conflict changes the future in unexpected ways.**

We all have hopes that one day society will be united. We have hopes of justice and equality. But what if that day never comes? What if that day comes, and we cannot see it? What if that day has come and gone, and it is not what we expected?

The Divide reveals our dependency on God to make changes for us by miraculously proving one side right and the other side wrong. We have hopes it will change the future and give us unity.

Change happens in the future when wrongs are righted. Dependencies are created on beliefs that others will right their wrongs to make our life better. The only way to make your life better is by taking responsibility for righting your own wrongs. It will change your future and give you control over your life.

Conflict, by its very nature, is divisive. It takes more than God and maturity to end it. Both sides need to be willing to make sacrifices to resolve it, and that is not always possible. Sometimes the things we fight for are things we need. That is a battle that never ends.

God cannot unite people who are determined to fight for what they want. God unites people based on what they need. He teaches us how to communicate our needs and to end the battles with the sins and neglect that divide us.

The Divide is a lesson for our survival. It is not evil. The neglect leading up to it is. Our responsibilities in life are not defined by rewards and punishments. They are defined by our needs and abilities, as human beings, to do the right thing.

We cannot change The Divide or forget it exists. We can only change the way we see it. Conflict changes the future in unexpected ways. In the past, rewards and punishments were outcomes that taught us right from wrong. Now, in the future, the promise of a reward and the threat of a punishment have become manipulations to produce a desired outcome.

Manipulations have expanded The Divide way past class, race, gender, and religion. It is creeping into families and relationships.

When we do not get what we want, we fight over it. We believe rewards and punishments are necessary to make changes that will hold it all together. In reality, it is robbing us of our humanity and faith.

That is where God's plan fits into our lives. Anyone who knows God knows He has a plan. God knows we do not always do the right thing. He sees it. That is why His plan includes teaching us how to believe in Him for our sanity. There are consequences for sin and neglect that we learn to see through the things we want.

God warned society, a long time ago, that we would become divided and suffer indefinitely if we lacked faith in Him, and He was right. We are warned about the future long before it happens. Knowledge of the future and God's power over it has been passed down through our ancestors for many generations. It is knowledge that is often ignored, hiding in the back of our minds and buried in our souls.

Each and every one of us has responsibilities in life. We have legal and moral responsibilities. We have relationship and financial responsibilities. We have responsibility for our safety and security. We have the responsibility for getting an education and learning how to satisfy our individual needs. We have a responsibility to adapt to all the changes that happen and do not happen in our lives.

Social responsibilities are only part of all the expectations others have of us. Ignoring them allows sin and neglect to create a future that threatens society's safety and security. It does not just prevent us from getting what we want. It puts us at risk.

Society needs to trust your judgments. Regardless of what is going on in life, our needs and responsibilities will not change in the future. Insecurities cause our responsibilities to become a struggle, even overwhelming at times. That pain triggers a need for comfort. It is where our hopes of change come from.

We tend to turn to immorality or doing the wrong thing to reward ourselves when our responsibilities cause us to feel deprived and neglected. It makes us feel more like ourselves. Those are not inhibitions we are casting off. We are freeing ourselves from our responsibilities in life.

Hopes of change mean changes need to happen inside of you. Rather than rewarding yourself, learn something. Empower yourself. Read a book. Challenge your mind. Raise your intelligence. Expand your imagination. Learn the secrets hiding in the future. What will happen in your future if you deprive yourself of humanity, morality, maturity, and independence?

God hides in the future with secrets of His own. God created The Divide through our beliefs in Him to show us the dark, punishing side of His nature. God uses The Divide to show us how He can and will deprive and neglect us as punishments for our sins and neglect.

We have a history of learning to fear and respect God or to despise Him. Those feelings toward God influence the choices we make and the way we treat others. God teaches us humanity, morality, maturity, and independence. They are social responsibilities that lead us to unity and equality. They are powers that dig up knowledge hiding inside each and every one of us that can be used to end the battles leading to The Divide.

Conflict gives us an opportunity to learn social responsibilities or to manipulate an outcome. When conflict gets in the way of what we want, that is the time to get control over ourselves, to make sacrifices, and walk away from a fight — even if means walking into our fears.

Self-control is a social skill that makes a difference in our future. Struggles are the outcomes, or consequences, of responsibilities. They require commitment. It is difficult to commit to our responsibilities when we are always finding ways to escape them.

We run from our responsibilities because of disappointment and anger over shattered hopes, or because of the desperation and anxiety that follow failure and rejection. It is easy to justify running away and hiding from responsibilities in life when we are scared and hurting. But what are we running into? Insanity?

This book, *Sins of Neglect*, leads you through the journey to insanity. It provides you with the causes of mental illness. Some common forms of mental illness are defined as depression, anxiety, bipolar disorder, and schizophrenia. In the past, insanity was the future that followed inhumanity, immorality, immaturity, and dependency.

The insanity that hides in the future is caused by knowledge that has been distorted by lies, dishonesty, and manipulations. We need truth and honesty that is found in humanity, morality, maturity, and independence to provide rationalizations and clarity for the life-altering choices we make. Sin and neglect cause confusion, leaving us unprepared for the future.

The truth and honesty change everything. They change you, your relationships, your life, and your future. They change your mind, your emotions, and the events that play out in your imagination. They change what happens inside of you and around you.

The truth and honesty give us knowledge that leads to sanity. It *needs* to change your beliefs about the future too, and it is your responsibility to do that. Avoid hiding the future you foresee in your imagination just because it is not what you want to see. Learn to be honest, beginning with yourself. It leads to your sanity.

You will make choices that are wrong for you. You will misjudge and trust people who cannot be trusted. You will fear things you do not need to fear. You will feel pressured into making choices that are wrong for you and right for others. You will get confused and not know what to do.

Humans have been experiencing confusion for generations. You would think we would know how to deal with it by now. But it is difficult to cope with something when we lack the ability to rationalize our choices. Confusion is not a generational thing that can be conquered with conflict. It is a human experience that lessens with maturity and doing the right thing every step of the way.

Most people do not see the struggles or pain that confusion can cause until they actually experience it for themselves. Confusion can become extremely discomforting and debilitating. Wrong choices intensify it to the point that we think we are going crazy. We need the clarity that comes from focusing on our needs and responsibilities. It gives us comfort that is difficult to see in times of confusion and despair.

The true cause of insanity is not a simple answer. The path to insanity is difficult to foresee. You see the path to insanity when you get there and have no idea how you got there. Everything seems like a blur. Your whole past seems like a repeat of yesterday.

Insanity and neglect do not magically resolve themselves in the future. Nor do the problems that follow them. Insanity is a troubled reality fraught with endless battles playing out in your imagination that make it extremely difficult to get control over yourself. Mental illness causes dysfunction and damage that hides in the future. Your whole, unforeseeable future can be wasted on repairing that damage.

ABOUT THE AUTHOR

Lily Abraham began her writing career after a decade studying the teachings of religion. Her research especially focused on the undeniable relationship between God and human nature. In addition, she has spent years examining and studying how our beliefs affect our choices, and the consequences in our lives and relationships. Her work is devoted to encouraging and creating an awareness of the influence God has over our everyday lives. She lives in Gilbert, Arizona.

www.ingramcontent.com/pod-product-compliance
Lightning Source LLC
Chambersburg PA
CBHW050638300426
44112CB00012B/1844